THIS BOOK BELONGS TO

_____

START DATE

_____

**SHE READS TRUTH**

**EXECUTIVE**

FOUNDER/CHIEF EXECUTIVE OFFICER
Raechel Myers

CO-FOUNDER/CHIEF CONTENT OFFICER
Amanda Bible Williams

CHIEF OPERATING OFFICER
Ryan Myers

ASSISTANT TO THE EXECUTIVES
Taura Ryan

OFFICE MANAGER
Nicole Quirion

**EDITORIAL**

EDITORIAL DIRECTOR
Jessica Lamb

MANAGING EDITOR
Beth Joseph, MDiv

DIGITAL MANAGING EDITOR
Oghosa Iyamu, MDiv

ASSOCIATE EDITORS
Lindsey Jacobi, MDiv
Tameshia Williams, ThM

EDITORIAL ASSISTANT
Hannah Little, MTS

**MARKETING**

CUSTOMER JOURNEY
MARKETING MANAGER
Megan Gibbs

PRODUCT MARKETING MANAGER
Wesley Chandler

SOCIAL MEDIA STRATEGIST
Taylor Krupp

**CREATIVE**

INTERIM CREATIVE DIRECTOR
Neely Tabor

ART DIRECTORS
Kelsea Allen
Aimee Lindamood

DESIGNERS
Abbey Benson
Amanda Brush, MA
Annie Glover
Lauren Haag

**LOGISTICS**

LOGISTICS DIRECTOR
Lauren Gloyne

PROJECT ASSISTANT
Mary Beth Montgomery

**SHIPPING**

SHIPPING MANAGER
Elizabeth Thomas

FULFILLMENT LEAD
Cait Baggerman

FULFILLMENT SPECIALISTS
Kajsa Matheny
Ashley Richardson
Noe Sanchez

SUBSCRIPTION INQUIRIES
orders@shereadstruth.com

**COMMUNITY SUPPORT**

COMMUNITY SUPPORT MANAGER
Kara Hewett, MOL

COMMUNITY SUPPORT SPECIALISTS
Katy McKnight
Heather Vollono
Margot Williams

**CONTRIBUTORS**

PHOTOGRAPHY
Annie Heath (99, 157)
Abigail Lewis (Cover, 24, 35, 66, 73, 117, 130, 164)

RECIPES
Alyssa Bethke (46, 110, 142)

**@SHEREADSTRUTH**

Download the
She Reads Truth app,
available for iOS
and Android

Subscribe to the
She Reads Truth podcast

**SHEREADSTRUTH.COM**

**SHE READS TRUTH™**

© 2022 by She Reads Truth, LLC

All rights reserved.

All photography used by permission.

ISBN 978-1-952670-55-8

1 2 3 4 5 6 7 8 9 10

Unless otherwise noted, all Scripture is taken from the Christian Standard Bible®. Copyright © 2020 by Holman Bible Publishers. Used by permission. Christian Standard Bible® and CSB® are federally registered trademarks of Holman Bible Publishers.

Scripture quotations marked NIV are taken from the Holy Bible, New International Version®, NIV®. Copyright © 1973, 1978, 1984, 2011 by Biblica, Inc.™ Used by permission of Zondervan. All rights reserved worldwide. www.zondervan.com. The "NIV" and "New International Version" are trademarks registered in the United States Patent and Trademark Office by Biblica, Inc.™

Recipes from *Satisfied* by Alyssa J Bethke, copyright © 2021. Reprinted by permission of Worthy Books, an imprint of Hachette Book Group, Inc.

Research support provided by Logos Bible Software™. Learn more at logos.com.

This book was printed offset in Nashville, Tennessee, on 70# Lynx Opaque. Cover is Neenah Classic Eggshell Solar White 80C.

THIS IS THE CHURCH

Our sense of identity
almost always informs
what we do.

Raechel Myers
FOUNDER & CHIEF
EXECUTIVE OFFICER

I've been a part of some pretty audacious things in my life, but sitting down with the She Reads Truth team to create a Bible reading plan that states, "This is the Church" feels like it might top them all.

*Where do we even begin?* How can we cover the breadth and depth of this between-two-advents body of believers across millenia and ethnicities and cultures and languages and denominations and personal convictions? What does unity look like in such a beautifully diverse community? In many ways, we were overwhelmed by the task.

But this is what I love about the work we do at She Reads Truth. We know where to begin. We start by setting aside what we think—even what we think we know—and we ask what the Bible says. If we had set out to create a five-week book about what we wanted to say about the Church, *then* tried to find Scripture to support every point, we would have failed. Instead, we read. And read and read and read. We looked at why the Church was founded, what it's called to be and do, and what it will become. My goodness, do we love what came together!

In an early conversation about this book, I asked our editorial team what they hoped for you as you experience this study. "We want her to know her identity within the people of God, and for her identity to inform her practice." *Yes! That's what I want, too!* And that's the thing. Our sense of identity almost always informs what we do. This is why knowing who the Bible says we are matters so much. And this is what we hope you will find as you read God's words about His Church.

As you read the curated scriptures in this book, my prayer is that you will see the beauty of the Church in a new way. That you will see it for what it was and is meant to be: set apart, the bride and body of Christ, the household of faith, the firstfruits of the new creation, commissioned by Christ to proclaim the Word, to be a people in progress, and to persevere as a people of remembrance and a gospel community. I pray that you will see and appreciate the unique diversity and unity of Christ's Church—the hope of the world!

Friends, let's spend the next five weeks as a community of women in the Word of God every day, finding our identity first as the family of God, the capital-C Church. (I think you're going to love the extra called "The Church & the World" on page 94!) And, with a newfound or newly resolved identity within the body of Christ, when someone asks us, or we need to remind each other, we can point to God's Word and answer, "This is the Church."

## DESIGN ON PURPOSE

At She Reads Truth, we believe in pairing the inherently beautiful Word of God with the aesthetic beauty it deserves. Each of our resources is thoughtfully and artfully designed to highlight the beauty, goodness, and truth of Scripture in a way that reflects the themes of each curated reading plan.

We drew inspiration for this Study Book from the design of our *This Is the Gospel* book. The reality of the gospel dictates the identity, calling, and mission of the Church. As a result, many of *This Is the Gospel*'s design features are intentionally echoed here. The branch featured on the cover is a nod to the illustrations used to represent the gospel narrative, and the same fonts are used throughout both Study Books.

The photos were purposefully selected for their depiction of shadows, high-contrast textures, and juxtaposition. These remind us of the many dual realities of the Church—it is visible and invisible, local and global, spiritual and physical (more on that on page 15). A warm and colorful palette is woven throughout to highlight the beauty and abundance we find in gospel community.

We're also excited to feature recipes from Alyssa Bethke's book *Satisfied*. These recipes are shareable and inviting! We hope they provide the opportunity to connect with others around a table, demonstrating our gospel response in community.

# HOW TO USE THIS BOOK

She Reads Truth is a community of women dedicated to reading the
Word of God every day. In the **This Is the Church** reading plan, we
will look at what the New Testament says about the Church, along with
complementary passages from the Old Testament, to see how the Church
is a new people unified in Christ to live out His mission on earth.

## READ & REFLECT

Your **This Is the Church** Study
Book focuses primarily on
Scripture, with bonus resources
to facilitate deeper engagement
with God's Word.

### SCRIPTURE READING

Designed for a Monday start,
this Study Book presents daily
readings on the identity and role
of the Church.

### REFLECTION

Each week features repeated questions
and space for personal reflection.

## COMMUNITY & CONVERSATION

You can start reading this book at any time! If
you want to join women from Dover to Denmark
as they read along with you, the She Reads Truth
community will start Day 1 of **This Is the Church**
on Monday, June 6, 2022.

 ## SHE READS TRUTH APP

For added community and conversation, join us in the
**This Is the Church** reading plan on the She Reads Truth
app. You can use the app to participate in community
discussion, download free lock screens for Weekly Truth
memorization, and more.

GRACE DAY

Use Saturdays to catch up on your reading, pray, and rest in the presence of the Lord.

WEEKLY TRUTH

Sundays are set aside for Scripture memorization.

*See tips for memorizing Scripture on page 182.*

EXTRAS

This book features additional tools to help you gain a deeper understanding of the text.

*Find a complete list of extras on page 13.*

 SHEREADSTRUTH.COM

The **This Is the Church** reading plan will also be available at SheReadsTruth.com as the community reads each day. Invite your family, friends, and neighbors to read along with you!

 SHE READS TRUTH PODCAST

Subscribe to the She Reads Truth podcast and join our founders and their guests each week as they talk about the beauty, goodness, and truth they find in Scripture.

 *Podcast episodes 131–135 for our* **This Is the Church** *series release on Mondays beginning June 6, 2022.*

# Table of Contents

Each weekday in this reading plan completes the statement, "The Church is..." as we explore the different facets of the identity and practices of the Church.

*The Church is...*

*The Church is...*

## Extras

## Recipes

# INTRODUCTION

There is one body and one Spirit—just as you were called to one hope at your calling—one Lord, one faith, one baptism, one God and Father of all, who is above all and through all and in all.

*Ephesians 4:4–6*

## WHAT IS THE CHURCH?

### 1

The Church is a community of people who are followers of Jesus Christ. It is unlike any other institution, club, meeting, network, or affiliation. The Church is the new covenant people of God, created by the gospel. (We'll read on Day 1 what it means that we are the people of God.)

## THE CHURCH IS...

### 2

*visible, global, and local.*

It is all those throughout the world who confess that Jesus is Lord. It includes believers from a broad spectrum of denominations and traditions, from diverse nationalities, ethnicities, and socioeconomic statuses, with different worship practices. It is not a building or specific location, but a worldwide collection of smaller groups of believers in our contemporary day and age. These smaller, essential assemblies are the local church.

*invisible and historic.*

This is the universal Church—all people in all places throughout time who are united in love for God, relationship with Christ, and life in the Spirit. It includes believers who have already died and those who are still living today.

*holy and imperfect.*

The Church, imperfect but made beautiful in Christ, is set apart as a gift to both followers of Jesus and those who don't yet know Him. It consists of flawed, sinful people who have fallen and will continue to fall short as we are made more and more like Christ through the work of the Holy Spirit.

## IN THIS READING PLAN

### 3

Rather than looking at how specific denominations and traditions structure the local church, we'll spend our time as a community reading Scripture about the nature, purpose, mission, and function of the broader Christian Church.

In the first week we'll explore how the Church is the people of God, established by Jesus as a unified, holy community living in response to the gospel and awaiting Christ's return. Each subsequent reading day is rooted in each of these foundational truths about the Church.

In the following weeks, we'll read metaphors that help us better understand what it means to be part of the Church. We'll also read about practices that shape the Church and what it looks like to continue the mission of Christ as His body on earth. Throughout, we'll see how our identity shapes our behavior and how our behavior, in turn, demonstrates and shapes our identity.

"

We must cease to think of the Church as a gathering of institutions and organisations, and we must get back this notion that we are the people of God.

—D. MARTYN LLOYD-JONES

"

ASIA

*379 million
Christians*

OCEANIA

*28 million
Christians*

*Data from "Christians by continent, 2020" in World Christian Encyclopedia, 3rd ed.*

KEY

APPROXIMATE NUMBER
OF GLOBAL CHRISTIANS

NORTH
AMERICA

268 million
Christians

EUROPE

565 million
Christians

LATIN
AMERICA

612 million
Christians

AFRICA

667 million
Christians

MAP

# GLOBAL CHRISTIANITY

OPEN TO SEE MAP ⟶

As Christians, we may belong to a local gathering of believers (a church), but we also are part of the global, historic Church that stretches beyond borders and spans the centuries. Scripture teaches that all followers of Jesus are our brothers and sisters in Christ. In the fold-out, we've included a map showing the approximate number of Christians around the world today.

We've also included a few facts below about the location of the women and men reading God's Word with She Reads Truth and He Reads Truth alongside you!

| Top International Countries for Shes & Hes | Top U.S. States for Shes & Hes |
|---|---|
| 1  CANADA | 1  TEXAS |
| 2  AUSTRALIA | 2  CALIFORNIA |
| 3  UNITED KINGDOM | 3  TENNESSEE |
| 4  NEW ZEALAND | 4  NORTH CAROLINA |
| 5  SINGAPORE | 5  GEORGIA |

# THE PEOPLE OF GOD

*Day 1*

*God's people are all those who know Him by faith. Everyone reconciled to God in Christ shares in this legacy of faith as Abraham's spiritual descendants, regardless of ethnicity or nationality.*

## ROMANS 9:6–8, 14–26, 30–33

[6] Now it is not as though the word of God has failed, because not all who are descended from Israel are Israel. [7] Neither is it the case that all of Abraham's children are his descendants. On the contrary, your offspring will be traced through Isaac. [8] That is, it is not the children by physical descent who are God's children, but the children of the promise are considered to be the offspring.

…

[14] What should we say then? Is there injustice with God? Absolutely not! [15] For he tells Moses, I will show mercy to whom I will show mercy, and I will have compassion on whom I will have compassion. [16] So then, it does not depend on human will or effort but on God who shows mercy. [17] For the Scripture tells Pharaoh, I raised you up for this reason so that I may display my power in you and that my name may be proclaimed in the whole earth. [18] So then, he has mercy on whom he wants to have mercy and he hardens whom he wants to harden.

[19] You will say to me, therefore, "Why then does he still find fault? For who resists his will?" [20] On the contrary, who are you, a human being, to talk back to God? Will what is formed say to the one who formed it, "Why did you make me like this?" [21] Or has the potter no right over the clay, to make from the same lump one piece of pottery for honor and another for dishonor? [22] And what if God, wanting to display his wrath and to make his power known, endured with much patience objects of wrath prepared for destruction? [23] And what if he did this to make known the riches of his glory on objects of mercy that he prepared beforehand for glory— [24] on us, the ones he also called, not only from the Jews but also from the Gentiles? [25] As it also says in Hosea,

I will call Not My People, My People,
and she who is Unloved, Beloved.

<sup>26</sup> And it will be in the place where they were told,
you are not my people,
there they will be called sons of the living God.

…

<sup>30</sup> What should we say then? Gentiles, who did not pursue righteousness, have obtained righteousness—namely the righteousness that comes from faith. <sup>31</sup> But Israel, pursuing the law of righteousness, has not achieved the righteousness of the law. <sup>32</sup> Why is that? Because they did not pursue it by faith, but as if it were by works. They stumbled over the stumbling stone. <sup>33</sup> As it is written,

Look, I am putting a stone in Zion to stumble over
and a rock to trip over,
and the one who believes on him
will not be put to shame.

## HEBREWS 11
*Living by Faith*

<sup>1</sup> Now faith is the reality of what is hoped for, the proof of what is not seen. <sup>2</sup> For by this our ancestors were approved.

<sup>3</sup> By faith we understand that the universe was created by the word of God, so that what is seen was made from things that are not visible.

<sup>4</sup> By faith Abel offered to God a better sacrifice than Cain did. By faith he was approved as a righteous man, because God approved his gifts, and even though he is dead, he still speaks through his faith.

<sup>5</sup> By faith Enoch was taken away, and so he did not experience death. He was not to be found because God took him away. For before he was taken away, he was approved as one who pleased God. <sup>6</sup> Now without faith it is impossible to please God, since the one who draws near to him must believe that he exists and that he rewards those who seek him.

<sup>7</sup> By faith Noah, after he was warned about what was not yet seen and motivated by godly fear, built an ark to deliver his family. By faith he condemned the world and became an heir of the righteousness that comes by faith.

<sup>8</sup> By faith Abraham, when he was called, obeyed and set out for a place that he was going to receive as an inheritance. He went out, even though he did not know where he was going. <sup>9</sup> By faith he stayed as a foreigner in the land of promise, living in tents as did Isaac and Jacob, coheirs of the same promise. <sup>10</sup> For he was looking forward to the city that has foundations, whose architect and builder is God.

<sup>11</sup> By faith even Sarah herself, when she was unable to have children, received power to conceive offspring, even though she was past the age, since she considered that the one who had promised was faithful.

<sup>12</sup> Therefore, from one man— in fact, from one as good as dead—came offspring as numerous as the stars of the sky and as innumerable as the grains of sand along the seashore.

<sup>13</sup> These all died in faith, although they had not received the things that were promised. But they saw them from a distance, greeted them, and confessed that they were foreigners and temporary residents on the earth. <sup>14</sup> Now those who say such things make it clear that they are seeking a homeland. <sup>15</sup> If they were thinking about where they came from, they would have had an opportunity to return. <sup>16</sup> But they now desire a better place—a heavenly one. Therefore, God is not ashamed to be called their God, for he has prepared a city for them.

<sup>17</sup> By faith Abraham, when he was tested, offered up Isaac. He received the promises and yet he was offering his one and only son, <sup>18</sup> the one to whom it had been said, Your offspring will be traced through Isaac. <sup>19</sup> He considered God to be able even to raise someone from the dead; therefore, he received him back, figuratively speaking.

20 By faith Isaac blessed Jacob and Esau concerning things to come. 21 By faith Jacob, when he was dying, blessed each of the sons of Joseph, and he worshiped, leaning on the top of his staff. 22 By faith Joseph, as he was nearing the end of his life, mentioned the exodus of the Israelites and gave instructions concerning his bones.

23 By faith Moses, after he was born, was hidden by his parents for three months, because they saw that the child was beautiful, and they didn't fear the king's edict. 24 By faith Moses, when he had grown up, refused to be called the son of Pharaoh's daughter 25 and chose to suffer with the people of God rather than to enjoy the fleeting pleasure of sin. 26 For he considered reproach for the sake of Christ to be greater wealth than the treasures of Egypt, since he was looking ahead to the reward.

27 By faith he left Egypt behind, not being afraid of the king's anger, for Moses persevered as one who sees him who is invisible. 28 By faith he instituted the Passover and the sprinkling of the blood, so that the destroyer of the firstborn might not touch the Israelites. 29 By faith they crossed the Red Sea as though they were on dry land. When the Egyptians attempted to do this, they were drowned.

30 By faith the walls of Jericho fell down after being marched around by the Israelites for seven days. 31 By faith Rahab the prostitute welcomed the spies in peace and didn't perish with those who disobeyed.

32 And what more can I say? Time is too short for me to tell about Gideon, Barak, Samson, Jephthah, David, Samuel, and the prophets, 33 who by faith conquered kingdoms, administered justice, obtained promises, shut the mouths of lions, 34 quenched the raging of fire, escaped the edge of the sword, gained strength in weakness, became mighty in battle, and put foreign armies to flight. 35 Women received their dead, raised to life again. Other people were tortured, not accepting release, so that they might gain a better resurrection. 36 Others experienced mockings and scourgings, as well as bonds and imprisonment. 37 They were stoned, they were sawed in two, they died by the sword, they wandered about in sheepskins, in goatskins, destitute, afflicted, and mistreated. 38 The world was not worthy of them. They wandered in deserts and on mountains, hiding in caves and holes in the ground.

39 All these were approved through their faith, but they did not receive what was promised, 40 since God had provided something better for us, so that they would not be made perfect without us.

## 2 TIMOTHY 2:19

Nevertheless, God's solid foundation stands firm, bearing this inscription: The Lord knows those who are his, and let everyone who calls on the name of the Lord turn away from wickedness.

## 1 PETER 2:9–10

9 But you are a chosen race, a royal priesthood, a holy nation, a people for his possession, so that you may proclaim the praises of the one who called you out of darkness into his marvelous light. 10 Once you were not a people, but now you are God's people; you had not received mercy, but now you have received mercy.

# *Notes*

_____

*Date*

THE CHURCH IS

# ESTABLISHED BY JESUS

*The Church was established by Jesus, is sustained by Jesus,
and rests on Him as its foundation.*

*Day 2*

*You who were far away have been brought near by the blood of Christ.*

---

## ISAIAH 49:6

…he says,
"It is not enough for you to be my servant
raising up the tribes of Jacob
and restoring the protected ones of Israel.
I will also make you a light for the nations,
to be my salvation to the ends of the earth."

## EPHESIANS 2:1-13

*From Death to Life*

[1] And you were dead in your trespasses and sins [2] in which you previously walked according to the ways of this world, according to the ruler of the power of the air, the spirit now working in the disobedient. [3] We too all previously lived among them in our fleshly desires, carrying out the inclinations of our flesh and thoughts, and we were by nature children under wrath as the others were also. [4] But God, who is rich in mercy, because of his great love that he had for us, [5] made us alive with Christ even though we were dead in trespasses. You are saved by grace! [6] He also raised us up with him and seated us with him in the heavens in Christ Jesus, [7] so that in the coming ages he might display the immeasurable riches of his grace through his kindness to us in Christ Jesus. [8] For you are saved by grace through faith, and this is not from yourselves; it is God's gift—

[9] not from works, so that no one can boast. [10] For we are his workmanship, created in Christ Jesus for good works, which God prepared ahead of time for us to do.

*Unity in Christ*

[11] So, then, remember that at one time you were Gentiles in the flesh—called "the uncircumcised" by those called "the circumcised," which is done in the flesh by human hands. [12] At that time you were without Christ, excluded from the citizenship of Israel, and foreigners to the covenants of promise, without hope and without God in the world. [13] But now in Christ Jesus, you who were far away have been brought near by the blood of Christ.

## MATTHEW 16:13-18

*Peter's Confession of the Messiah*

[13] When Jesus came to the region of Caesarea Philippi, he asked his disciples, "Who do people say that the Son of Man is?"

[14] They replied, "Some say John the Baptist; others, Elijah; still others, Jeremiah or one of the prophets."

[15] "But you," he asked them, "who do you say that I am?"

¹⁶ Simon Peter answered, "You are the Messiah, the Son of the living God."

¹⁷ Jesus responded, "Blessed are you, Simon son of Jonah, because flesh and blood did not reveal this to you, but my Father in heaven. ¹⁸ And I also say to you that you are Peter, and on this rock I will build my church, and the gates of Hades will not overpower it."

## HEBREWS 8:6–13

⁶ But Jesus has now obtained a superior ministry, and to that degree he is the mediator of a better covenant, which has been established on better promises.

*A Superior Covenant*

⁷ For if that first covenant had been faultless, there would have been no occasion for a second one. ⁸ But finding fault with his people, he says:

> See, the days are coming, says the Lord,
> when I will make a new covenant
> with the house of Israel
> and with the house of Judah—
> ⁹ not like the covenant
> that I made with their ancestors
> on the day I took them by the hand
> to lead them out of the land of Egypt.
> I showed no concern for them, says the Lord,
> because they did not continue in my covenant.
> ¹⁰ For this is the covenant
> that I will make with the house of Israel
> after those days, says the Lord:
> I will put my laws into their minds
> and write them on their hearts.
> I will be their God,
> and they will be my people.
> ¹¹ And each person will not teach his fellow citizen,
> and each his brother or sister, saying, "Know the Lord,"
> because they will all know me,
> from the least to the greatest of them.
> ¹² For I will forgive their wrongdoing,
> and I will never again remember their sins.

¹³ By saying a new covenant, he has declared that the first is obsolete. And what is obsolete and growing old is about to pass away.

## HEBREWS 9:11–15

*New Covenant Ministry*

¹¹ But Christ has appeared as a high priest of the good things that have come. In the greater and more perfect tabernacle not made with hands (that is, not of this creation), ¹² he entered the most holy place once for all time, not by the blood of goats and calves, but by his own blood, having obtained eternal redemption. ¹³ For if the blood of goats and bulls and the ashes of a young cow, sprinkling those who are defiled, sanctify for the purification of the flesh, ¹⁴ how much more will the blood of Christ, who through the eternal Spirit offered himself without blemish to God, cleanse our consciences from dead works so that we can serve the living God?

¹⁵ Therefore, he is the mediator of a new covenant, so that those who are called might receive the promise of the eternal inheritance, because a death has taken place for redemption from the transgressions committed under the first covenant.

## 1 CORINTHIANS 3:11

For no one can lay any foundation other than what has been laid down. That foundation is Jesus Christ.

# Notes

_____

*Date*

DAY 3

*The Church is*

# UNITED
# IN CHRIST

*Followers of Jesus Christ are called to pursue oneness as we remain connected to our Triune God, the source, sustainer, and perfect example of unity.*

## JOHN 17:20–26
*Jesus Prays for All Believers*

[20] "I pray not only for these, but also for those who believe in me through their word. [21] May they all be one, as you, Father, are in me and I am in you. May they also be in us, so that the world may believe you sent me. [22] I have given them the glory you have given me, so that they may be one as we are one. [23] I am in them and you are in me, so that they may be made completely one, that the world may know you have sent me and have loved them as you have loved me.

[24] "Father, I want those you have given me to be with me where I am, so that they will see my glory, which you have given me because you loved me before the world's foundation. [25] Righteous Father, the world has not known you. However, I have known you, and they have known that you sent me. [26] I made your name known to them and will continue to make it known, so that the love you have loved me with may be in them and I may be in them."

## EPHESIANS 4:1–6
*Unity and Diversity in the Body of Christ*

[1] Therefore I, the prisoner in the Lord, urge you to walk worthy of the calling you have received, [2] with all humility and gentleness, with patience, bearing with one another in love, [3] making every effort to keep the unity of the Spirit through the bond of peace.

[4] There is one body and one Spirit—just as you were called to one hope at your calling— [5] one Lord, one faith, one baptism, [6] one God and Father of all, who is above all and through all and in all.

## GALATIANS 3:28

There is no Jew or Greek, slave or free, male and female; since you are all one in Christ Jesus.

# Unity and Diversity of Belief

The scriptures we are reading today call the Church to be one in Christ, united with one another as we are reconciled to God through Christ. This can be true even as Christians are a part of a wide variety of local churches and traditions. We can find unity in the absolutes of shared Christian identity and mission despite differences in secondary and tertiary issues.

Reflect on where your different beliefs fall based on the categories below. Keep these categories in mind as you read through this plan and engage with the family of God in your local church and beyond.

---

### 1 ESSENTIALS

Beliefs that define what it means to be a Christan. (See "What Is the Gospel?" on p. 32.)

---

### 2 NON-ESSENTIALS

Matters of importance that Scripture speaks to but Christians disagree on how to interpret or apply. Differences in these secondary beliefs are what distinguish most denominations or traditions.

---

### 3 OPINIONS

Areas of preference or extrapolation beyond Scripture. Though these are relevant to the Christian life, Christians even within local congregations may disagree.

## 1 CORINTHIANS 1:10–13
### Divisions at Corinth

[10] Now I urge you, brothers and sisters, in the name of our Lord Jesus Christ, that all of you agree in what you say, that there be no divisions among you, and that you be united with the same understanding and the same conviction. [11] For it has been reported to me about you, my brothers and sisters, by members of Chloe's people, that there is rivalry among you. [12] What I am saying is this: One of you says, "I belong to Paul," or "I belong to Apollos," or "I belong to Cephas," or "I belong to Christ." [13] Is Christ divided? Was Paul crucified for you? Or were you baptized in Paul's name?

## 1 CORINTHIANS 12:13

For we were all baptized by one Spirit into one body—whether Jews or Greeks, whether slaves or free—and we were all given one Spirit to drink.

## PHILIPPIANS 2:1–4
### Christian Humility

[1] If, then, there is any encouragement in Christ, if any consolation of love, if any fellowship with the Spirit, if any affection and mercy, [2] make my joy complete by thinking the same way, having the same love, united in spirit, intent on one purpose. [3] Do nothing out of selfish ambition or conceit, but in humility consider others as more important than yourselves. [4] Everyone should look not to his own interests, but rather to the interests of others.

## ROMANS 15:5–6

[5] Now may the God who gives endurance and encouragement grant you to live in harmony with one another, according to Christ Jesus, [6] so that you may glorify the God and Father of our Lord Jesus Christ with one mind and one voice.

## REVELATION 7:9–17

[9] After this I looked, and there was a vast multitude from every nation, tribe, people, and language, which no one could number, standing before the throne and before the Lamb. They were clothed in white robes with palm branches in their hands. [10] And they cried out in a loud voice:

> Salvation belongs to our God,
> who is seated on the throne,
> and to the Lamb!

[11] All the angels stood around the throne, and along with the elders and the four living creatures they fell facedown before the throne and worshiped God, [12] saying,

> Amen! Blessing and glory and wisdom
> and thanksgiving and honor
> and power and strength
> be to our God forever and ever. Amen.

[13] Then one of the elders asked me, "Who are these people in white robes, and where did they come from?"

[14] I said to him, "Sir, you know."

Then he told me: These are the ones coming out of the great tribulation. They washed their robes and made them white in the blood of the Lamb.

> [15] For this reason they are before the throne of God,
> and they serve him day and night in his temple.
> The one seated on the throne will shelter them:
> [16] They will no longer hunger;
> they will no longer thirst;
> the sun will no longer strike them,
> nor will any scorching heat.
> [17] For the Lamb who is at the center of the throne
> will shepherd them;
> he will guide them to springs of the waters of life,
> and God will wipe away every tear from their eyes.

# WHAT IS THE GOSPEL?

The *gospel*, or "good news," is what Jesus Christ has done to restore broken creation and sinful people to their holy Creator. It is the true story of our relationship with God, which was marred by sin and is restored by grace through faith in Christ alone. It is this gospel that creates a gospel community, the Church. The gospel can be summarized in four parts: creation, fall, redemption, and restoration.

## Creation

God is the infinite, eternal Creator of all things.
HEB 11:3

God created the heavens and the earth and declared that His creation was "good."
GN 1:1, 31

God created humanity in His own image and likeness.
GN 1:27

God created humanity to love, obey, worship, and be in a relationship with Him.
1CO 8:6

## Fall

Adam and Eve, the first humans, turned away from God and rebelled against Him.
GN 3:1–7

When Adam and Eve rebelled against God, all creation became subject to death, decay, and frustration.
RM 8:20–22

We all have inherited this sinful nature, and we are unable to obey God perfectly.
IS 53:6

The penalty for sin is death, and we are unable to save ourselves.
RM 6:23

# Redemption

God responded to our need for salvation by sending His only Son, Jesus Christ, to live among us.
1 JN 4:14

Jesus delivers us from sin and condemnation and offers us eternal life with God.
JN 3:16–18

Jesus lived, died, and rose from the dead as the perfect substitute for all who believe in Him.
1 PT 2:24

We are saved by grace through faith in Jesus.
EPH 2:6–9

# Restoration

Jesus reconciles us to God by securing our relationship with God forever. We receive Christ's righteousness and are presented as holy and blameless before God.
COL 1:21–22

Christians play a role in God's restoring work in the world through loving and serving both God and others.
MT 5:16

The Holy Spirit transforms us into the image of Christ.
2 CO 3:18

One day all God's people and all creation will be perfectly restored, and Jesus will make everything new.
RV 21:1–5

The Church is

# SET APART
# IN CHRIST

---

*In Christ, the people of the Church are holy, set apart for a purpose.*
*We are called to pursue lives of holiness as a changed people.*

## 1 PETER 1:13-20
*A Call to Holy Living*

[13] Therefore, with your minds ready for action, be sober-minded and set your hope completely on the grace to be brought to you at the revelation of Jesus Christ. [14] As obedient children, do not be conformed to the desires of your former ignorance. [15] But as the one who called you is holy, you also are to be holy in all your conduct; [16] for it is written, Be holy, because I am holy. [17] If you appeal to the Father who judges impartially according to each one's work, you are to conduct yourselves in reverence during your time living as strangers. [18] For you know that you were redeemed from your empty way of life inherited from your ancestors, not with perishable things like silver or gold, [19] but with the precious blood of Christ, like that of an unblemished and spotless lamb. [20] He was foreknown before the foundation of the world but was revealed in these last times for you.

## 2 TIMOTHY 1:9

He has saved us and called us with a holy calling, not according to our works, but according to his own purpose and grace, which was given to us in Christ Jesus before time began.

## 1 JOHN 1:5-10
*Fellowship with God*

[5] This is the message we have heard from him and declare to you: God is light, and there is absolutely no darkness in him. [6] If we say, "We have fellowship with him," and yet we walk in darkness, we are lying and are not practicing the truth. [7] If we walk in the light as he himself is in the light, we have fellowship with one another, and the blood of Jesus his Son cleanses us from all sin. [8] If we say, "We have no sin," we are deceiving ourselves, and the truth is not in us. [9] If we confess our sins, he is faithful and righteous to forgive us our sins and to cleanse us from all unrighteousness. [10] If we say, "We have not sinned," we make him a liar, and his word is not in us.

## 1 JOHN 2:1-6

[1] My little children, I am writing you these things so that you may not sin. But if anyone does sin, we have an advocate with the Father—Jesus Christ the righteous one. [2] He himself is the atoning sacrifice for our sins, and not only for ours, but also for those of the whole world.

*God's Commands*

[3] This is how we know that we know him: if we keep his commands. [4] The one who says, "I have come to know him," and yet doesn't keep his commands, is a liar, and the truth is not in him. [5] But whoever keeps his word, truly in him the love of God is made complete. This is how we know we are in him: [6] The one who says he remains in him should walk just as he walked.

## 1 JOHN 3:7-10

[7] Little children, let no one deceive you. The one who does what is right is righteous, just as he is righteous. [8] The one who commits sin is of the devil, for the devil has sinned from the beginning. The Son of God was revealed for this purpose: to destroy the devil's works. [9] Everyone who has been born of God does not sin, because his seed remains in him; he is not able to sin, because he has been born of God. [10] This is how God's children and the devil's children become obvious. Whoever does not do what is right is not of God, especially the one who does not love his brother or sister.

## ROMANS 8:29

For those he foreknew he also predestined to be conformed to the image of his Son, so that he would be the firstborn among many brothers and sisters.

## EPHESIANS 5:1-17

[1] Therefore, be imitators of God, as dearly loved children, [2] and walk in love, as Christ also loved us and gave himself for us, a sacrificial and fragrant offering to God. [3] But sexual immorality and any impurity or greed should not even be heard of among you, as is proper for saints. [4] Obscene and

foolish talking or crude joking are not suitable, but rather giving thanks. [5] For know and recognize this: Every sexually immoral or impure or greedy person, who is an idolater, does not have an inheritance in the kingdom of Christ and of God.

*Light Versus Darkness*

[6] Let no one deceive you with empty arguments, for God's wrath is coming on the disobedient because of these things. [7] Therefore, do not become their partners.

[8] For you were once darkness, but now you are light in the Lord. Walk as children of light— [9] for the fruit of the light consists of all goodness, righteousness, and truth—

[10] testing what is pleasing to the Lord. [11] Don't participate in the fruitless works of darkness, but instead expose them. [12] For it is shameful even to mention what is done by them in secret. [13] Everything exposed by the light is made visible, [14] for what makes everything visible is light. Therefore it is said:

> Get up, sleeper, and rise up from the dead,
> and Christ will shine on you.

*Consistency in the Christian Life*

[15] Pay careful attention, then, to how you walk—not as unwise people but as wise— [16] making the most of the time, because the days are evil. [17] So don't be foolish, but understand what the Lord's will is.

LEVITICUS 20:26

"You are to be holy to me because I, the Lord, am holy, and I have set you apart from the nations to be mine."

ISAIAH 26:2

Open the gates
so a righteous nation can come in—
one that remains faithful.

*The Church is*

# WAITING AND PREPARING

The Church exists in response to Jesus's first coming and continues on in anticipation of His promised return. Through all circumstances we are called to live in such a way that our present faith and obedience reflect our future, glorious hope.

JOHN 14:1-3

¹ "Don't let your heart be troubled. Believe in God; believe also in me. ² In my Father's house are many rooms. If it were not so, would I have told you that I am going to prepare a place for you?

³ If I go away and prepare a place for you, I will come again and take you to myself, so that where I am you may be also."

TITUS 2:11-13

¹¹ For the grace of God has appeared, bringing salvation for all people, ¹² instructing us to deny godlessness and worldly lusts and to live in a sensible, righteous, and godly way in the present age, ¹³ while we wait for the blessed hope, the appearing of the glory of our great God and Savior, Jesus Christ.

MATTHEW 25:1-13

*The Parable of the Ten Virgins*

¹ "At that time the kingdom of heaven will be like ten virgins who took their lamps and went out to meet the groom. ² Five of them were foolish and five were wise. ³ When the foolish took their lamps, they didn't take oil with them; ⁴ but the wise ones took oil in their flasks with their lamps. ⁵ When the groom was delayed, they all became drowsy and fell asleep.

⁶ "In the middle of the night there was a shout: 'Here's the groom! Come out to meet him.'

⁷ "Then all the virgins got up and trimmed their lamps. ⁸ The foolish ones said to the wise ones, 'Give us some of your oil, because our lamps are going out.'

⁹ "The wise ones answered, 'No, there won't be enough for us and for you. Go instead to those who sell oil, and buy some for yourselves.'

¹⁰ "When they had gone to buy some, the groom arrived, and those who were ready went in with him to the wedding banquet, and the door was shut. ¹¹ Later the rest of the virgins also came and said, 'Master, master, open up for us!'

¹² "He replied, 'Truly I tell you, I don't know you!'

¹³ "Therefore be alert, because you don't know either the day or the hour."

[8] Dear friends, don't overlook this one fact: With the Lord one day is like a thousand years, and a thousand years like one day. [9] The Lord does not delay his promise, as some understand delay, but is patient with you, not wanting any to perish but all to come to repentance.

[10] But the day of the Lord will come like a thief; on that day the heavens will pass away with a loud noise, the elements will burn and be dissolved, and the earth and the works on it will be disclosed. [11] Since all these things are to be dissolved in this way, it is clear what sort of people you should be in holy conduct and godliness [12] as you wait for the day of God and hasten its coming. Because of that day, the heavens will be dissolved with fire and the elements will melt with heat. [13] But based on his promise, we wait for new heavens and a new earth, where righteousness dwells.

JAMES 5:7-8

*Waiting for the Lord*

[7] Therefore, brothers and sisters, be patient until the Lord's coming. See how the farmer waits for the precious fruit of the earth and is patient with it until it receives the early and the late rains. [8] You also must be patient. Strengthen your hearts, because the Lord's coming is near.

PSALM 130:5-6

[5] I wait for the LORD; I wait
and put my hope in his word.
[6] I wait for the Lord
more than watchmen for the morning—
more than watchmen for the morning.

# Notes

*Date*

WEEK 1

# RESPONSE

*The Church is...*

THE PEOPLE OF GOD

ESTABLISHED BY JESUS

UNITED IN CHRIST

SET APART IN CHRIST

WAITING AND PREPARING

Use these questions as a guide for reflecting on this week's reading. You may not have a response for each one—that's okay!

What truths about the
Church stood out to you?

_____

What comforted or
encouraged you?

_____

What challenged you?

_____

What questions do you have
that you want to explore?

_____

What action might you need
to take in response to what
you read this week? What is
your first step?

_____

1

2

3

4

5

# FELLOWSHIP
# AT THE TABLE

In the first century, table fellowship represented fellowship before God, where everyone breaking bread together shared in the blessing spoken over the meal. For the early Church, it symbolized the family believers belong to regardless of social status and cultural background.

Still today, gathering together around a table for a meal is an opportunity like few others to cross both social and cultural barriers to build a connection with others. Prepare, serve, and share these recipes (see pages 46, 110, and 142) as a reminder of how the gospel brings unlikely people together in community.

# Strawberry Cake

PREP TIME: 20 MINUTES
COOK TIME: 23–28 MINUTES
SERVES: 12

## INGREDIENTS

*Cake*

1 (15¼-ounce) package white cake mix,
plus 3 tablespoons flour*

1 (3-ounce) package strawberry Jell-O® instant
gelatin mix (dry powder)

4 large eggs

1 cup canola oil**

⅔ cup fresh strawberries, hulled and mashed***

½ cup water

*Frosting*

½ cup (1 stick) unsalted butter, slightly softened

4¼ cups powdered sugar

⅓ cup fresh strawberries, hulled and mashed***

*Optional Garnish*

Fresh strawberries

## INSTRUCTIONS

Preheat oven to 325°F if you have darker metal or
nonstick pans, or to 350°F for glass or shiny metal
pans. Use 2 (9-inch) cake pans. Line the bottom of
each pan with parchment paper (trace the bottom
of the cake pan on the parchment, cut out, and
place in the cake pan).

*For the cake*

In a large bowl, combine all ingredients until
moistened, then beat with an electric mixer for
2 minutes on medium speed. Divide the batter
evenly between prepared cake pans.

Bake for 23 to 28 minutes. Don't overbake—
the cakes are done when a toothpick inserted
in the center comes out clean. The cakes may
look slightly browned around the edges but the
top should be mostly pink. Remove cakes from
oven and let sit for 10 minutes. Carefully run a
knife around the edges and turn out the layers
onto cooling racks. Let cool before assembling
and frosting.

*For the frosting*

While the cakes bake, set butter on counter until
slightly softened. Beat the butter, powdered sugar,
and strawberries with an electric mixer until
smooth. If your frosting is too soft, chill it for
10 minutes and then gently stir before assembling
and frosting the layers. If desired, garnish with
2 to 3 strawberries.

## NOTES

*For a gluten-free cake, use a 22-ounce package of King Arthur™ Gluten-Free Yellow Cake Mix
and 3 tablespoons of King Arthur™ Gluten-Free Measure for Measure Flour.

**Organic coconut oil or SunCoco made for baking and high-heat cooking can be substituted for
canola oil.

***You'll need about 12 ounces of fresh strawberries to get the total of 1 cup of mashed berries.
You can also thaw and mash frozen, unsweetened strawberries instead of using fresh—you'll need
about 12 ounces of frozen berries.

# Grace Day

*Take this day to catch up on your reading, pray, and rest in the presence of the Lord.*

"YOU ARE TO BE HOLY TO ME BECAUSE I, THE LORD, AM HOLY, AND I HAVE SET YOU APART FROM THE NATIONS TO BE MINE."

*Leviticus 20:26*

*Weekly Truth*

*Scripture is God-breathed and true. When we memorize it,
we carry the good news of Jesus with us wherever we go.*

*Over the course of this Study Book, we will memorize Ephesians
4:1–6, where Paul calls his fellow believers to live in unity as the
body of Christ. This week, let's memorize the first verse.*

Therefore I, the prisoner in the Lord, urge you to walk worthy of the calling you have received, with all humility and gentleness, with patience, bearing with one another in love, making every effort to keep the unity of the Spirit through the bond of peace. There is one body and one Spirit—just as you were called to one hope at your calling—one Lord, one faith, one baptism, one God and Father of all, who is above all and through all and in all.

EPHESIANS 4:1–6

*See tips for memorizing Scripture on page 182.*

*The Church is*

# THE BRIDE
# OF CHRIST

---

*Scripture illustrates the relationship between Christ and His Church through the imagery of a wedding. As the bridegroom, Christ loves, provides for, and sacrifices Himself for His bride, who responds to His love in preparation and submission.*

*Consistency in the Christian Life*

¹⁵ Pay careful attention, then, to how you walk—not as unwise people but as wise— ¹⁶ making the most of the time, because the days are evil. ¹⁷ So don't be foolish, but understand what the Lord's will is. ¹⁸ And don't get drunk with wine, which leads to reckless living, but be filled by the Spirit: ¹⁹ speaking to one another in psalms, hymns, and spiritual songs, singing and making music with your heart to the Lord, ²⁰ giving thanks always for everything to God the Father in the name of our Lord Jesus Christ, ²¹ submitting to one another in the fear of Christ.

*Wives and Husbands*

²² Wives, submit to your husbands as to the Lord, ²³ because the husband is the head of the wife as Christ is the head of the church. He is the Savior of the body. ²⁴ Now as the church submits to Christ, so also wives are to submit to their husbands in everything. ²⁵ Husbands, love your wives,

just as Christ loved the church and gave himself for her ²⁶ to make her holy, cleansing her with the washing of water by the word.

²⁷ He did this to present the church to himself in splendor, without spot or wrinkle or anything like that, but holy and blameless. ²⁸ In the same way, husbands are to love their wives as their own bodies. He who loves his wife loves himself. ²⁹ For no one ever hates his own flesh but provides and cares for it, just as Christ does for the church, ³⁰ since we are members of his body. ³¹ For this reason a man will leave his father and mother and be joined to his wife, and the two will become one flesh. ³² This mystery is profound, but I am talking about Christ and the church.

⁶ Then I heard something like the voice of a vast multitude, like the sound of cascading waters, and like the rumbling of loud thunder, saying,

Hallelujah, because our Lord God, the Almighty,
reigns!
⁷ Let us be glad, rejoice, and give him glory,
because the marriage of the Lamb has come,
and his bride has prepared herself.
⁸ She was given fine linen to wear, bright and pure.

For the fine linen represents the righteous acts of the saints.

⁹ Then he said to me, "Write: Blessed are those invited to the marriage feast of the Lamb!" He also said to me, "These words of God are true."

## REVELATION 21:2-11

² I also saw the holy city, the new Jerusalem, coming down out of heaven from God, prepared like a bride adorned for her husband.

³ Then I heard a loud voice from the throne: Look, God's dwelling is with humanity, and he will live with them. They will be his peoples, and God himself will be with them and will be their God. ⁴ He will wipe away every tear from their eyes. Death will be no more; grief, crying, and pain will be no more, because the previous things have passed away.

⁵ Then the one seated on the throne said, "Look, I am making everything new." He also said, "Write, because these words are faithful and true." ⁶ Then he said to me, "It is done! I am the Alpha and the Omega, the beginning and the end. I will freely give to the thirsty from the spring of the water of life. ⁷ The one who conquers will inherit these things, and I will be his God, and he will be my son. ⁸ But the cowards, faithless, detestable, murderers, sexually immoral, sorcerers, idolaters, and all liars—their share will be in the lake that burns with fire and sulfur, which is the second death."

*The New Jerusalem*

⁹ Then one of the seven angels, who had held the seven bowls filled with the seven last plagues, came and spoke with me: "Come, I will show you the bride, the wife of the Lamb." ¹⁰ He then carried me away in the Spirit to a great, high mountain and showed me the holy city, Jerusalem, coming down out of heaven from God, ¹¹ arrayed with God's glory. Her radiance was like a precious jewel, like a jasper stone, clear as crystal.

## REVELATION 22:17, 20

¹⁷ Both the Spirit and the bride say, "Come!" Let anyone who hears, say, "Come!" Let the one who is thirsty come. Let the one who desires take the water of life freely.

. . .

²⁰ He who testifies about these things says, "Yes, I am coming soon."

Amen! Come, Lord Jesus!

# Notes

_____

*Date*

"

Thus the very purpose of His self-giving on the cross was not just to save isolated individuals, and so perpetuate their loneliness, but to create a new community whose members would belong to Him, love one another, and eagerly serve the world.

—JOHN STOTT

"

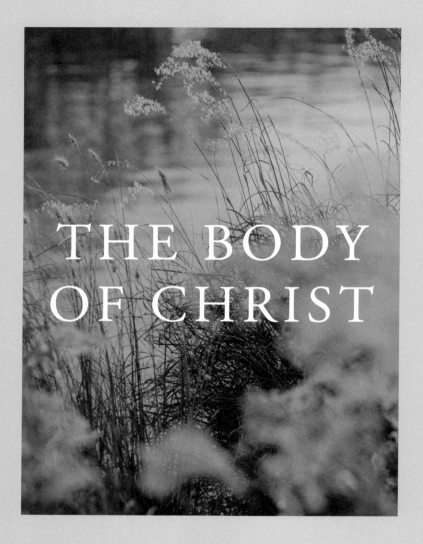

# THE BODY OF CHRIST

*Paul uses a metaphor of the human body to describe the relationship between Christ and the Church. As the head of the body, Christ unifies the individual parts that serve distinct purposes.*

*Day 9*

*He is also the head of the body, the church.*

---

EPHESIANS 1:20–23

*God's Power in Christ*

[20] He exercised this power in Christ by raising him from the dead and seating him at his right hand in the heavens— [21] far above every ruler and authority, power and dominion, and every title given, not only in this age but also in the one to come. [22] And he subjected everything under his feet and appointed him as head over everything for the church, [23] which is his body, the fullness of the one who fills all things in every way.

COLOSSIANS 1:18

He is also the head of the body, the church;
he is the beginning,
the firstborn from the dead,
so that he might come to have
first place in everything.

EPHESIANS 4:15–16

[15] But speaking the truth in love, let us grow in every way into him who is the head—Christ. [16] From him the whole body, fitted and knit together by every supporting ligament, promotes the growth of the body for building itself up in love by the proper working of each individual part.

1 CORINTHIANS 12:12–27

*Unity Yet Diversity in the Body*

[12] For just as the body is one and has many parts, and all the parts of that body, though many, are one body—so also is Christ. [13] For we were all baptized by one Spirit into one body—whether Jews or Greeks, whether slaves or free—and we were all given one Spirit to drink. [14] Indeed, the body is not one part but many. [15] If the foot should say, "Because I'm not a hand, I don't belong to the body," it is not for that reason any less a part of the body. [16] And if the ear should say, "Because I'm not an eye, I don't belong to the body," it is not for that reason any less a part of the body. [17] If the whole body were an eye, where would the hearing be? If the whole body were an ear, where would the sense of smell be? [18] But as it is, God has arranged each one of the parts in the body just as he wanted. [19] And if they were all the same part, where would the body be? [20] As it is, there are many parts, but one body. [21] The eye cannot say to the hand, "I don't need you!" Or again, the head can't say to the feet, "I don't need you!" [22] On the contrary, those parts of the body that are weaker are indispensable. [23] And those parts of the body that we consider less honorable, we clothe these with greater honor, and our unrespectable parts are treated with greater respect, [24] which our respectable parts do not need.

Instead, God has put the body together, giving greater honor to the less honorable, [25] so that there would be no division in the body, but that the members would have the same concern for each other. [26] So if one member suffers, all the members suffer with it; if one member is honored, all the members rejoice with it.

## [27] Now you are the body of Christ, and individual members of it.

### COLOSSIANS 2:9–15

[9] For the entire fullness of God's nature dwells bodily in Christ, [10] and you have been filled by him, who is the head over every ruler and authority. [11] You were also circumcised in him with a circumcision not done with hands, by putting off the body of flesh, in the circumcision of Christ, [12] when you were buried with him in baptism, in which you were also raised with him through faith in the working of God, who raised him from the dead. [13] And when you were dead in trespasses and in the uncircumcision of your flesh, he made you alive with him and forgave us all our trespasses. [14] He erased the certificate of debt, with its obligations, that was against us and opposed to us, and has taken it away by nailing it to the cross. [15] He disarmed the rulers and authorities and disgraced them publicly; he triumphed over them in him.

### ROMANS 12:4–5

[4] Now as we have many parts in one body, and all the parts do not have the same function, [5] in the same way we who are many are one body in Christ and individually members of one another.

# Notes

_____

*Date*

# THE SHEPHERD'S FLOCK

*Day 10*

*Jesus's love for the Church is expressed through the imagery of a perfect shepherd and his flock. Unlike the negligent shepherds who previously led God's people, Jesus delights to search for, gather, and tend to His flock, even laying down His life for His sheep.*

## EZEKIEL 34

*The Shepherds and God's Flock*

1 The word of the LORD came to me: 2 "Son of man, prophesy against the shepherds of Israel. Prophesy, and say to them, 'This is what the Lord GOD says to the shepherds: Woe to the shepherds of Israel, who have been feeding themselves! Shouldn't the shepherds feed their flock? 3 You eat the fat, wear the wool, and butcher the fattened animals, but you do not tend the flock. 4 You have not strengthened the weak, healed the sick, bandaged the injured, brought back the strays, or sought the lost. Instead, you have ruled them with violence and cruelty. 5 They were scattered for lack of a shepherd; they became food for all the wild animals when they were scattered. 6 My flock went astray on all the mountains and every high hill. My flock was scattered over the whole face of the earth, and there was no one searching or seeking for them.

7 "'Therefore, you shepherds, hear the word of the LORD. 8 As I live—this is the declaration of the Lord GOD—because my flock, lacking a shepherd, has become prey and food for every wild animal, and because my shepherds do not search for my flock, and because the shepherds feed themselves rather than my flock, 9 therefore, you shepherds, hear the word of the LORD!

10 "'This is what the Lord GOD says: Look, I am against the shepherds. I will demand my flock from them and prevent them from shepherding the flock. The shepherds will no longer feed themselves, for I will rescue my flock from their mouths so that they will not be food for them.

11 "'For this is what the Lord GOD says: See, I myself will search for my flock and look for them. 12 As a shepherd looks

for his sheep on the day he is among his scattered flock, so I will look for my flock. I will rescue them from all the places where they have been scattered on a day of clouds and total darkness. ¹³ I will bring them out from the peoples, gather them from the countries, and bring them to their own soil. I will shepherd them on the mountains of Israel, in the ravines, and in all the inhabited places of the land. ¹⁴ I will tend them in good pasture, and their grazing place will be on Israel's lofty mountains. There they will lie down in a good grazing place; they will feed in rich pasture on the mountains of Israel. ¹⁵ I will tend my flock and let them lie down. This is the declaration of the Lord God.

¹⁶ I will seek the lost, bring back the strays, bandage the injured, and strengthen the weak,

but I will destroy the fat and the strong. I will shepherd them with justice.

¹⁷ "'As for you, my flock, the Lord God says this: Look, I am going to judge between one sheep and another, between the rams and goats. ¹⁸ Isn't it enough for you to feed on the good pasture? Must you also trample the rest of the pasture with your feet? Or isn't it enough that you drink the clear water? Must you also muddy the rest with your feet? ¹⁹ Yet my flock has to feed on what your feet have trampled, and drink what your feet have muddied.

²⁰ "'Therefore, this is what the Lord God says to them: See, I myself will judge between the fat sheep and the lean sheep. ²¹ Since you have pushed with flank and shoulder and butted all the weak ones with your horns until you scattered them all over, ²² I will save my flock. They will no longer be prey, and I will judge between one sheep and another. ²³ I will establish over them one shepherd, my servant David, and he will shepherd them. He will tend them himself and will be their shepherd. ²⁴ I, the Lord, will be their God, and my servant David will be a prince among them. I, the Lord, have spoken.

²⁵ "'I will make a covenant of peace with them and eliminate dangerous creatures from the land, so that they may live securely in the wilderness and sleep in the forest. ²⁶ I will make them and the area around my hill a blessing: I will send down showers in their season; they will be showers of blessing. ²⁷ The trees of the field will yield their fruit, and the land will yield its produce; my flock will be secure in their land. They will know that I am the Lord when I break the bars of their yoke and rescue them from the power of those who enslave them. ²⁸ They will no longer be prey for the nations, and the wild creatures of the earth will not consume them. They will live securely, and no one will frighten them. ²⁹ I will establish for them a place renowned for its agriculture, and they will no longer be victims of famine in the land. They will no longer endure the insults of the nations. ³⁰ Then they will know that I, the Lord their God, am with them, and that they, the house of Israel, are my people. This is the declaration of the Lord God. ³¹ You are my flock, the human flock of my pasture, and I am your God. This is the declaration of the Lord God.'"

"I will indeed gather all of you, Jacob;
I will collect the remnant of Israel.
I will bring them together like sheep in a pen,
like a flock in the middle of its pasture.
It will be noisy with people."

JOHN 10:7-18, 27-30

[7] Jesus said again, "Truly I tell you, I am the gate for the sheep. [8] All who came before me are thieves and robbers, but the sheep didn't listen to them. [9] I am the gate. If anyone enters by me, he will be saved and will come in and go out and find pasture. [10] A thief comes only to steal and kill and destroy. I have come so that they may have life and have it in abundance.

[11] "I am the good shepherd. The good shepherd lays down his life for the sheep.

[12] The hired hand, since he is not the shepherd and doesn't own the sheep, leaves them and runs away when he sees a wolf coming. The wolf then snatches and scatters them. [13] This happens because he is a hired hand and doesn't care about the sheep.

[14] "I am the good shepherd. I know my own, and my own know me, [15] just as the Father knows me, and I know the Father. I lay down my life for the sheep. [16] But I have other sheep that are not from this sheep pen; I must bring them also, and they will listen to my voice. Then there will be one flock, one shepherd. [17] This is why the Father loves me, because I lay down my life so that I may take it up again. [18] No one takes it from me, but I lay it down on my own. I have the right to lay it down, and I have the right to take it up again. I have received this command from my Father."

…

[27] "My sheep hear my voice, I know them, and they follow me. [28] I give them eternal life, and they will never perish. No one will snatch them out of my hand. [29] My Father, who has given them to me, is greater than all. No one is able to snatch them out of the Father's hand. [30] I and the Father are one."

LUKE 12:31-32

[31] "But seek his kingdom, and these things will be provided for you. [32] Don't be afraid, little flock, because your Father delights to give you the kingdom."

# Notes

Date

THE CHURCH IS

# EMPOWERED BY THE HOLY SPIRIT

*The Holy Spirit fills and fuels the Church with God's power to preach the gospel, serve others, repent from sin, and increasingly live in freedom.*

*Day 11*

*The Holy Spirit Promised*

4 While he was with them, he commanded them not to leave Jerusalem, but to wait for the Father's promise. "Which," he said, "you have heard me speak about; 5 for John baptized with water, but you will be baptized with the Holy Spirit in a few days."

6 So when they had come together, they asked him, "Lord, are you restoring the kingdom to Israel at this time?"

7 He said to them, "It is not for you to know times or periods that the Father has set by his own authority.

8 But you will receive power when the Holy Spirit has come on you,

and you will be my witnesses in Jerusalem, in all Judea and Samaria, and to the ends of the earth."

LUKE 24:49

"And look, I am sending you what my Father promised. As for you, stay in the city until you are empowered from on high."

ACTS 2:1–21, 32–41
*Pentecost*

1 When the day of Pentecost had arrived, they were all together in one place. 2 Suddenly a sound like that of a violent rushing wind came from heaven, and it filled the whole house where they were staying. 3 They saw tongues like flames of fire that separated and rested on each one of them. 4 Then they were all filled with the Holy Spirit and began to speak in different tongues, as the Spirit enabled them.

5 Now there were Jews staying in Jerusalem, devout people from every nation under heaven. 6 When this sound occurred, a crowd came together and was confused because each one heard them speaking in his own language. 7 They were astounded and amazed, saying, "Look, aren't all these who are speaking Galileans? 8 How is it that each of us can hear them in our own native language? 9 Parthians, Medes,

Elamites; those who live in Mesopotamia, in Judea and Cappadocia, Pontus and Asia, 10 Phrygia and Pamphylia, Egypt and the parts of Libya near Cyrene; visitors from Rome (both Jews and converts), 11 Cretans and Arabs—we hear them declaring the magnificent acts of God in our own tongues." 12 They were all astounded and perplexed, saying to one another, "What does this mean?" 13 But some sneered and said, "They're drunk on new wine."

*Peter's Sermon*

14 Peter stood up with the Eleven, raised his voice, and proclaimed to them, "Fellow Jews and all you residents of Jerusalem, let this be known to you, and pay attention to my words. 15 For these people are not drunk, as you suppose, since it's only nine in the morning. 16 On the contrary, this is what was spoken through the prophet Joel:

17 And it will be in the last days, says God,
that I will pour out my Spirit on all people;
then your sons and your daughters will prophesy,
your young men will see visions,
and your old men will dream dreams.
18 I will even pour out my Spirit
on my servants in those days, both men and women
and they will prophesy.
19 I will display wonders in the heaven above
and signs on the earth below:
blood and fire and a cloud of smoke.
20 The sun will be turned to darkness
and the moon to blood
before the great and glorious day of the Lord comes.
21 Then everyone who calls
on the name of the Lord will be saved."

...

32 "God has raised this Jesus; we are all witnesses of this. 33 Therefore, since he has been exalted to the right hand of God and has received from the Father the promised Holy Spirit, he has poured out what you both see and hear. 34 For it was not David who ascended into the heavens, but he himself says:

The Lord declared to my Lord,
'Sit at my right hand
³⁵ until I make your enemies your footstool.'

³⁶ "Therefore let all the house of Israel know with certainty that God has made this Jesus, whom you crucified, both Lord and Messiah."

*Call to Repentance*

³⁷ When they heard this, they were pierced to the heart and said to Peter and the rest of the apostles, "Brothers, what should we do?"

³⁸ Peter replied, "Repent and be baptized, each of you, in the name of Jesus Christ for the forgiveness of your sins, and you will receive the gift of the Holy Spirit. ³⁹ For the promise is for you and for your children, and for all who are far off, as many as the Lord our God will call." ⁴⁰ With many other words he testified and strongly urged them, saying, "Be saved from this corrupt generation!" ⁴¹ So those who accepted his message were baptized, and that day about three thousand people were added to them.

## 1 CORINTHIANS 12:4–11

⁴ Now there are different gifts, but the same Spirit. ⁵ There are different ministries, but the same Lord. ⁶ And there are different activities, but the same God works all of them in each person. ⁷ A manifestation of the Spirit is given to each person for the common good: ⁸ to one is given a message of wisdom through the Spirit, to another, a message of knowledge by the same Spirit, ⁹ to another, faith by the same Spirit, to another, gifts of healing by the one Spirit, ¹⁰ to another, the performing of miracles, to another, prophecy, to another, distinguishing between spirits, to another, different kinds of tongues, to another, interpretation of tongues. ¹¹ One and the same Spirit is active in all these, distributing to each person as he wills.

## GALATIANS 5:25

If we live by the Spirit, let us also keep in step with the Spirit.

## EPHESIANS 1:13–14, 17–19

¹³ In him you also were sealed with the promised Holy Spirit when you heard the word of truth, the gospel of your salvation, and when you believed. ¹⁴ The Holy Spirit is the down payment of our inheritance, until the redemption of the possession, to the praise of his glory.

…

¹⁷ I pray that the God of our Lord Jesus Christ, the glorious Father, would give you the Spirit of wisdom and revelation in the knowledge of him. ¹⁸ I pray that the eyes of your heart may be enlightened so that you may know what is the hope of his calling, what is the wealth of his glorious inheritance in the saints, ¹⁹ and what is the immeasurable greatness of his power toward us who believe, according to the mighty working of his strength.

## TITUS 3:4–7

⁴ But when the kindness of God our Savior and his love for mankind appeared, ⁵ he saved us—not by works of righteousness that we had done, but according to his mercy—through the washing of regeneration and renewal by the Holy Spirit. ⁶ He poured out his Spirit on us abundantly through Jesus Christ our Savior ⁷ so that, having been justified by his grace, we may become heirs with the hope of eternal life.

# Notes

_____

*Date*

# SPIRITUAL GIFTS

Spiritual gifts are one way God equips the Church for the life and work He calls us to. These gifts range from essentials for the Christian life to miraculous abilities to roles and skills necessary for the ongoing ministry of the Church. While the gifts on this list vary in type, they all share one distinctive quality: they come from the Holy Spirit.

1    *Essential Gifts*

Qualities given to all believers everywhere that are necessary for living the Christian life.

2    *Dynamic Gifts*

Specific abilities given for the distinct purpose of delivering or validating a message from God.

3    *Functional Gifts*

Roles and abilities needed for the ongoing structure and ministry of the Church.

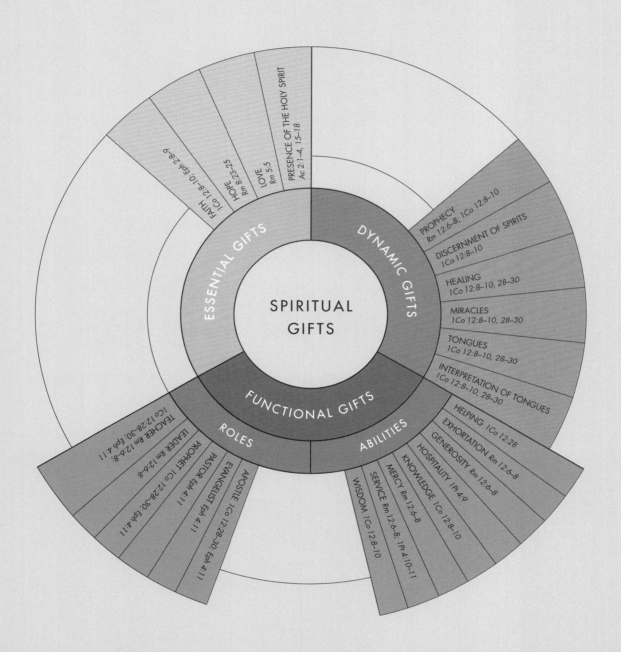

SPIRITUAL GIFTS

**ESSENTIAL GIFTS**
- FAITH 1Co 12:8–10; Eph 2:8–9
- HOPE Rm 8:23–25
- LOVE Rm 5:5
- PRESENCE OF THE HOLY SPIRIT Ac 2:1–4, 15–18

**DYNAMIC GIFTS**
- PROPHECY Rm 12:6–8; 1Co 12:8–10
- DISCERNMENT OF SPIRITS 1Co 12:8–10
- HEALING 1Co 12:8–10, 28–30
- MIRACLES 1Co 12:8–10, 28–30
- TONGUES 1Co 12:8–10, 28–30
- INTERPRETATION OF TONGUES 1Co 12:8–10, 28–30

**FUNCTIONAL GIFTS**

**ROLES**
- TEACHER Rm 12:6–8; 1Co 12:28–30; Eph 4:11
- LEADER Rm 12:6–8
- PROPHET 1Co 12:28–30; Eph 4:11
- PASTOR Eph 4:11
- EVANGELIST Eph 4:11
- APOSTLE 1Co 12:28–30; Eph 4:11

**ABILITIES**
- HELPING 1Co 12:28
- EXHORTATION Rm 12:6–8
- GENEROSITY Rm 12:6–8
- HOSPITALITY 1P 4:9
- KNOWLEDGE 1Co 12:8–10
- MERCY Rm 12:6–8
- SERVICE Rm 12:6–8; 1P 4:10–11
- WISDOM 1Co 12:8–10

*Some Christian traditions believe that the dynamic gifts ceased early in Church history. Others hold they still are accessible today.*

DAY 12

*The Church is*

# THE TEMPLE OF THE LIVING GOD

*God's dwelling place exists among His people, who are marked and set apart as holy.*

## 1 CORINTHIANS 3:9–17

[9] For we are God's coworkers. You are God's field, God's building.

[10] According to God's grace that was given to me, I have laid a foundation as a skilled master builder, and another builds on it. But each one is to be careful how he builds on it. [11] For no one can lay any foundation other than what has been laid down. That foundation is Jesus Christ. [12] If anyone builds on the foundation with gold, silver, costly stones, wood, hay, or straw, [13] each one's work will become obvious. For the day will disclose it, because it will be revealed by fire; the fire will test the quality of each one's work. [14] If anyone's work that he has built survives, he will receive a reward. [15] If anyone's work is burned up, he will experience loss, but he himself will be saved—but only as through fire.

[16] Don't you yourselves know that you are God's temple and that the Spirit of God lives in you? [17] If anyone destroys God's temple, God will destroy him; for

## God's temple is holy, and that is what you are.

## 1 CORINTHIANS 6:19–20

[19] Don't you know that your body is a temple of the Holy Spirit who is in you, whom you have from God? You are not your own, [20] for you were bought at a price. So glorify God with your body.

## 2 CORINTHIANS 6:16–18

[16] And what agreement does the temple of God have with idols? For we are the temple of the living God, as God said:

> I will dwell
> and walk among them,
> and I will be their God,
> and they will be my people.
> [17] Therefore, come out from among them
> and be separate, says the Lord;
> do not touch any unclean thing,
> and I will welcome you.
> [18] And I will be a Father to you,
> and you will be sons and daughters to me,
> says the Lord Almighty.

## EPHESIANS 2:19–22

<sup>19</sup> So, then, you are no longer foreigners and strangers, but fellow citizens with the saints, and members of God's household, <sup>20</sup> built on the foundation of the apostles and prophets, with Christ Jesus himself as the cornerstone. <sup>21</sup> In him the whole building, being put together, grows into a holy temple in the Lord. <sup>22</sup> In him you are also being built together for God's dwelling in the Spirit.

## REVELATION 21:15–27

<sup>15</sup> The one who spoke with me had a golden measuring rod to measure the city, its gates, and its wall. <sup>16</sup> The city is laid out in a square; its length and width are the same. He measured the city with the rod at 12,000 *stadia*. Its length, width, and height are equal. <sup>17</sup> Then he measured its wall, 144 cubits according to human measurement, which the angel used. <sup>18</sup> The building material of its wall was jasper, and the city was pure gold clear as glass. <sup>19</sup> The foundations of the city wall were adorned with every kind of jewel: the first foundation is jasper, the second sapphire, the third chalcedony, the fourth emerald, <sup>20</sup> the fifth sardonyx, the sixth carnelian, the seventh chrysolite, the eighth beryl, the ninth topaz, the tenth chrysoprase, the eleventh jacinth, the twelfth amethyst. <sup>21</sup> The twelve gates are twelve pearls; each individual gate was made of a single pearl. The main street of the city was pure gold, transparent as glass.

<sup>22</sup> I did not see a temple in it, because the Lord God the Almighty and the Lamb are its temple. <sup>23</sup> The city does not need the sun or the moon to shine on it, because the glory of God illuminates it, and its lamp is the Lamb. <sup>24</sup> The nations will walk by its light, and the kings of the earth will bring their glory into it. <sup>25</sup> Its gates will never close by day because it will never be night there. <sup>26</sup> They will bring the glory and honor of the nations into it. <sup>27</sup> Nothing unclean will ever enter it, nor anyone who does what is detestable or false, but only those written in the Lamb's book of life.

## ISAIAH 28:16

Therefore the Lord God said:
"Look, I have laid a stone in Zion,
a tested stone,
a precious cornerstone, a sure foundation;
the one who believes will be unshakable."

NOTES

# RESPONSE

*The Church is...*

**THE BRIDE OF CHRIST**

**THE BODY OF CHRIST**

**THE SHEPHERD'S FLOCK**

**EMPOWERED BY THE HOLY SPIRIT**

**THE TEMPLE OF THE LIVING GOD**

Use these questions as a guide for reflecting on this week's reading. You may not have a response for each one—that's okay!

What truths about the Church stood out to you?

_____

What comforted or encouraged you?

_____

What challenged you?

_____

What questions do you have that you want to explore?

_____

What action might you need to take in response to what you read this week? What is your first step?

_____

1

2

3

4

5

# Grace Day

*Take this day to catch up on your reading, pray, and rest in the presence of the Lord.*

"YOU ARE MY FLOCK, THE HUMAN FLOCK OF MY PASTURE, AND I AM YOUR GOD. THIS IS THE DECLARATION OF THE LORD GOD."

*Ezekiel 34:31*

DAY 14

*Weekly Truth*

Scripture is God-breathed and true. When we memorize it,
we carry the good news of Jesus with us wherever we go.

This week we will continue to memorize Ephesians 4:1–6,
by adding the next two verses, where Paul emphasizes unity
in the Spirit.

Therefore I, the prisoner in the Lord, urge you to walk worthy of the calling you have received, **with all humility and gentleness, with patience, bearing with one another in love, making every effort to keep the unity of the Spirit through the bond of peace.** There is one body and one Spirit—just as you were called to one hope at your calling—one Lord, one faith, one baptism, one God and Father of all, who is above all and through all and in all.

EPHESIANS 4:1–6

*See tips for memorizing Scripture on page 182.*

DAY 15

*The Church is*

# A ROYAL PRIESTHOOD

*The Church is a new priesthood, different from the priesthood of the Old Testament. Jesus Christ is our High Priest who leads us in offering our lives in worship as a living sacrifice to God.*

## 1 PETER 2:4–9

⁴ As you come to him, a living stone—rejected by people but chosen and honored by God— ⁵ you yourselves, as living stones, a spiritual house, are being built to be a holy priesthood to offer spiritual sacrifices acceptable to God through Jesus Christ. ⁶ For it stands in Scripture:

> See, I lay a stone in Zion,
> a chosen and honored cornerstone,
> and the one who believes in him
> will never be put to shame.

⁷ So honor will come to you who believe; but for the unbelieving,

> The stone that the builders rejected—
> this one has become the cornerstone,

⁸ and

> A stone to stumble over,
> and a rock to trip over.

They stumble because they disobey the word; they were destined for this.

⁹ But you are a chosen race, a royal priesthood, a holy nation, a people for his possession,

so that you may proclaim the praises of the one who called you out of darkness into his marvelous light.

## HEBREWS 7:22–28

²² Because of this oath, Jesus has also become the guarantee of a better covenant.

²³ Now many have become Levitical priests, since they are prevented by death from remaining in office. ²⁴ But because he remains forever, he holds his priesthood permanently. ²⁵ Therefore, he is able to save completely those who come to God through him, since he always lives to intercede for them.

²⁶ For this is the kind of high priest we need: holy, innocent, undefiled, separated from sinners, and exalted above the heavens. ²⁷ He doesn't need to offer sacrifices every day, as high priests do—first for their own sins, then for those of the people. He did this once for all time when he offered himself. ²⁸ For the law appoints as high priests men who are weak, but the promise of the oath, which came after the law, appoints a Son, who has been perfected forever.

## HEBREWS 8:1-2

[1] Now the main point of what is being said is this: We have this kind of high priest, who sat down at the right hand of the throne of the Majesty in the heavens, [2] a minister of the sanctuary and the true tabernacle that was set up by the Lord and not man.

## HEBREWS 10:19-22

*Exhortations to Godliness*

[19] Therefore, brothers and sisters, since we have boldness to enter the sanctuary through the blood of Jesus— [20] he has inaugurated for us a new and living way through the curtain (that is, through his flesh)— [21] and since we have a great high priest over the house of God, [22] let us draw near with a true heart in full assurance of faith, with our hearts sprinkled clean from an evil conscience and our bodies washed in pure water.

## HEBREWS 13:15

Therefore, through him let us continually offer up to God a sacrifice of praise, that is, the fruit of lips that confess his name.

## 2 CORINTHIANS 2:14-15

[14] But thanks be to God, who always leads us in Christ's triumphal procession and through us spreads the aroma of the knowledge of him in every place.

[15] For to God we are the fragrance of Christ among those who are being saved and among those who are perishing.

## ROMANS 12:1

Therefore, brothers and sisters, in view of the mercies of God, I urge you to present your bodies as a living sacrifice, holy and pleasing to God; this is your true worship.

## REVELATION 1:4-6

[4] John: To the seven churches in Asia. Grace and peace to you from the one who is, who was, and who is to come, and from the seven spirits before his throne, [5] and from Jesus Christ, the faithful witness, the firstborn from the dead and the ruler of the kings of the earth.

To him who loves us and has set us free from our sins by his blood, [6] and made us a kingdom, priests to his God and Father—to him be glory and dominion forever and ever. Amen.


REVELATION 5:10
You made them a kingdom
and priests to our God,
and they will reign on the earth.

*The Church is*

# THE HOUSEHOLD OF FAITH

---

*The Church is a spiritual family, God's household, made up of men, women, and children adopted as coheirs with Christ.*

## MATTHEW 12:46–50

*True Relationships*

46 While he was still speaking with the crowds, his mother and brothers were standing outside wanting to speak to him. 47 Someone told him, "Look, your mother and your brothers are standing outside, wanting to speak to you."

48 He replied to the one who was speaking to him, "Who is my mother and who are my brothers?" 49 Stretching out his hand toward his disciples, he said, "Here are my mother and my brothers! 50 For whoever does the will of my Father in heaven is my brother and sister and mother."

## JOHN 1:10–13

10 He was in the world, and the world was created through him, and yet the world did not recognize him. 11 He came to his own, and his own people did not receive him. 12 But to all who did receive him, he gave them the right to be children of God, to those who believe in his name, 13 who were born, not of natural descent, or of the will of the flesh, or of the will of man, but of God.

## EPHESIANS 1:3–6

*God's Rich Blessings*

3 Blessed is the God and Father of our Lord Jesus Christ, who has blessed us with every spiritual blessing in the heavens in Christ. 4 For he chose us in him, before the foundation of the world, to be holy and blameless in love before him. 5 He predestined us to be adopted as sons through Jesus Christ for himself, according to the good pleasure of his will, 6 to the praise of his glorious grace that he lavished on us in the Beloved One.

## 1 JOHN 3:1–2

1 See what great love the Father has given us that we should be called God's children—and we are! The reason the world does not know us is that it didn't know him. 2 Dear friends, we are God's children now, and what we will be has not yet been revealed. We know that when he appears, we will be like him because we will see him as he is.

## ROMANS 8:15–17

15 For you did not receive a spirit of slavery to fall back into fear. Instead, you received the Spirit of adoption, by whom we cry out, *"Abba,* Father!" 16 The Spirit himself testifies together with our spirit that we are God's children, 17 and if children, also heirs—heirs of God and coheirs with Christ— if indeed we suffer with him so that we may also be glorified with him.

## GALATIANS 3:24–26, 29

24 The law, then, was our guardian until Christ, so that we could be justified by faith. 25 But since that faith has come, we are no longer under a guardian, 26 for through faith you are all sons of God in Christ Jesus.

…

29 And if you belong to Christ, then you are Abraham's seed, heirs according to the promise.

## 1 TIMOTHY 3:15

But if I should be delayed, I have written so that you will know how people ought to conduct themselves in God's household, which is the church of the living God, the pillar and foundation of the truth.

# Notes

Date

The Church is

# THE FIRSTFRUITS OF THE NEW CREATION

*The Church is a display of Christ's active work in making all things new.
As citizens of the eternal kingdom of God, we live in this world yet long
for our true and eternal home.*

JOHN 17:1-19

*Jesus Prays for Himself*

¹ Jesus spoke these things, looked up to heaven, and said, "Father, the hour has come. Glorify your Son so that the Son may glorify you, ² since you gave him authority over all people, so that he may give eternal life to everyone you have given him. ³ This is eternal life: that they may know you, the only true God, and the one you have sent—Jesus Christ. ⁴ I have glorified you on the earth by completing the work you gave me to do. ⁵ Now, Father, glorify me in your presence with that glory I had with you before the world existed.

*Jesus Prays for His Disciples*

⁶ "I have revealed your name to the people you gave me from the world. They were yours, you gave them to me, and they have kept your word. ⁷ Now they know that everything you have given me is from you, ⁸ because I have given them the words you gave me. They have received them and have known for certain that I came from you. They have believed that you sent me.

⁹ "I pray for them. I am not praying for the world but for those you have given me, because they are yours. ¹⁰ Everything I have is yours, and everything you have is mine, and I am glorified in them. ¹¹ I am no longer in the world, but they are in the world, and I am coming to you. Holy Father, protect them by your name that you have given me, so that they may be one as we are one. ¹² While I was with them, I was protecting them by your name that you have given me. I guarded them and not one of them is lost, except the son of destruction, so that the Scripture may be fulfilled. ¹³ Now I am coming to you, and I speak these things in the world so that they may have my joy completed in them. ¹⁴ I have given them your word. The world hated them because they are not of the world, just as I am not of the world. ¹⁵ I am not praying that you take them out of the world but that you protect them from the evil one. ¹⁶ They are not of the world, just as I am not of the world. ¹⁷ Sanctify them by the truth; your word is truth. ¹⁸ As you sent me into the world, I also have sent them into the world. ¹⁹ I sanctify myself for them, so that they also may be sanctified by the truth."

JAMES 1:18

By his own choice, he gave us birth by the word of truth so that we would be a kind of firstfruits of his creatures.

PHILIPPIANS 3:20-21

²⁰ Our citizenship is in heaven, and we eagerly wait for a Savior from there, the Lord Jesus Christ. ²¹ He will transform the body of our humble condition into the likeness of his glorious body, by the power that enables him to subject everything to himself.

## 2 CORINTHIANS 5:1-9, 17
*Our Future After Death*

¹ For we know that if our earthly tent we live in is destroyed, we have a building from God, an eternal dwelling in the heavens, not made with hands. ² Indeed, we groan in this tent, desiring to put on our heavenly dwelling, ³ since, when we are clothed, we will not be found naked. ⁴ Indeed, we groan while we are in this tent, burdened as we are, because we do not want to be unclothed but clothed, so that mortality may be swallowed up by life. ⁵ Now the one who prepared us for this very purpose is God, who gave us the Spirit as a down payment.

⁶ So we are always confident and know that while we are at home in the body we are away from the Lord. ⁷ For we walk by faith, not by sight. ⁸ In fact, we are confident, and we would prefer to be away from the body and at home with the Lord. ⁹ Therefore, whether we are at home or away, we make it our aim to be pleasing to him.

…

¹⁷ Therefore, if anyone is in Christ, he is a new creation; the old has passed away, and see, the new has come!

## ROMANS 8:18-25
*From Groans to Glory*

¹⁸ For I consider that the sufferings of this present time are not worth comparing with the glory that is going to be revealed to us. ¹⁹ For the creation eagerly waits with anticipation for God's sons to be revealed. ²⁰ For the creation was subjected to futility—not willingly, but because of him who subjected it—in the hope ²¹ that the creation itself will also be set free from the bondage to decay into the glorious freedom of God's children. ²² For we know that the whole creation has been groaning together with labor pains until now. ²³ Not only that, but we ourselves who have the Spirit as the firstfruits—we also groan within ourselves, eagerly waiting for adoption, the redemption of our bodies. ²⁴ Now in this hope we were saved, but hope that is seen is not hope, because who hopes for what he sees? ²⁵ Now if we hope for what we do not see, we eagerly wait for it with patience.

# Notes

_____

*Date*

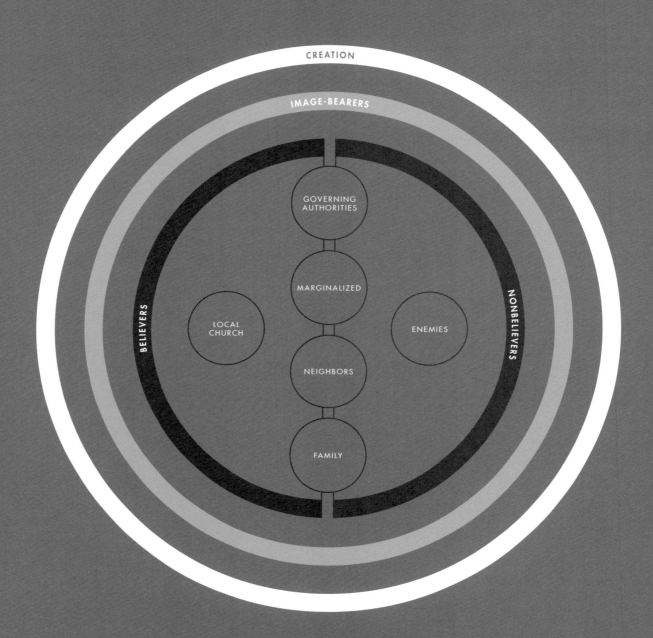

CREATION

IMAGE-BEARERS

BELIEVERS

NONBELIEVERS

GOVERNING AUTHORITIES

MARGINALIZED

LOCAL CHURCH

ENEMIES

NEIGHBORS

FAMILY

The Church & the World

God's people are called to think differently about every aspect of the world, from creation to the family unit to the local church and beyond. The following pages contain an overview of what Scripture says about the different ways Christians are called to interact with all God has made. The diagram on the opposite page depicts how these relationships build upon each other. As you read, take time to consider how each group is related to one another.

## CREATION

Of all His created beings, God has given humans a unique role as caretakers of the earth. As His image-bearers we share in this responsibility of stewardship, or caring for all of God's creation. Our work and calling, regardless of compensation or role, is to build and mend the world as an extension of God's work. We are called to tend to creation until all things are fully renewed when Jesus returns.

GN 1; 2:15; EX 23:10-11; LV 25:1-28; RV 11:18

## IMAGE-BEARERS

Every human being, regardless of age, race, economic class, or physical or mental ability, is made in the image of God. We have a responsibility to relate to all people, whether believers or nonbelievers, as those who bear this same image and are worthy of dignity and respect.

GN 1:26-28; 5:1-2; 9:1-5; JMS 3:9-10

## NONBELIEVERS

Followers of Jesus are called to not be isolated from those who don't know Christ. Rather, we are to demonstrate Christ's love in how we live and to share the good news of His life, death, and resurrection with others. Scripture also instructs us to use discernment in these relationships, remaining aware of the influence those who don't know Jesus can have in our lives.

MT 9:10-13; 28:19-20; JN 4:1-26; 2CO 6:14-17; COL 4:5-6

## BELIEVERS

Christians are connected to one another in Christ. We are called to live out our relationships with one another as a demonstration of the unity and love made possible in Jesus. Knowing that sin affects our relationships with one another, we attempt when possible "to live at peace with everyone."

JN 13:34–35; RM 12:10, 18; GL 5:13; EPH 4:32; COL 3:13

## LOCAL CHURCH

In addition to being part of the larger body of Christ around the world and across time, we also see examples in Scripture of Christians belonging to smaller groups of believers. In this context, we hold one another accountable through the teaching of God's Word and discipleship.

MT 18:15–20; AC 2:42–47; RM 12:3–8; JMS 5:13–18

## ENEMIES

Throughout life we will encounter those who oppose God, His plan, and His people. We are instructed to refrain from retaliating or seeking revenge against those who mistreat us or seek our harm. Instead, we are called to love our enemies, knowing that God is just and He is making all things new. While believers wait for this day, we speak out and stand against evil because all people are made in God's image and are worthy of both dignity and respect.

DT 31:6; 32:4; PS 1; PR 24:1–20; MT 5:38–40, 43–48; RM 12:17–21; EPH 5:11–12; 1PT 2:21–25; 3:9; RV 21:1–8

## GOVERNING AUTHORITIES

In almost every case, Christians are called to very simple instructions regarding governing authorities: obey and pray for those God has placed in authority. However, civil disobedience is called for when a believer would have to disobey God in order to obey governing authorities. As those who are in relationship with a good and just God, Christians are also called to stand against injustice.

PR 31:8–9; JR 22:1–5; DN 3; 6:1–10; AM 5:4–15; MK 12:17; AC 5:25–32; RM 13:1–2; 1TM 2:1–2; 1PT 2:13–14

## MARGINALIZED

Throughout the Old Testament, God gave instructions on the just and merciful treatment of those belonging to the most disempowered groups in society—the widow, the fatherless, the foreigner, the enslaved, and those with limited rights or who were oppressed. In the New Testament, Jesus ministered to these marginalized people across different categories, whether foreigners, disenfranchised social groups, or those suffering from illness or physical limitation. As followers of Christ, we are called to follow this example, showing special care and protection for the most vulnerable members of society.

DT 10:19; 15:12–18; IS 1:17; MT 25:31–40; LK 5:12–16; 9:46–48; JMS 1:27; 2:1–13

## NEIGHBORS

Jesus summed up the entirety of the Law in two commandments—love God and love your neighbor. We are to minister to our neighbors' needs, extending them the care we would show ourselves in any given situation.

LV 19:18; PR 3:29; LK 10:25–37; RM 13:9–10

## FAMILY

Familial relationships echo the relationship believers share with God: the institution of marriage reflects the relationship between Christ and the Church, and parent-child relationships reflect the relationship between God the Father and His children. As part of representing God's kingdom, we are called to live out family relationships with mutual honor, love, and sacrifice, while resisting the temptation to idolize these relationships over our commitment to Jesus. At the same time, Jesus challenges us to expand our understanding of family, extending the boundaries beyond the nuclear unit to include other believers as our brothers and sisters in Christ.

EX 20:12; MK 3:31–35; LK 14:25–26; JN 19:25–27; EPH 5:22–33; 6:1–4

*The Church is*

# COMMISSIONED BY CHRIST

---

*Christ calls His Church to herald the good news to each other,
our communities, and the world.*

## MATTHEW 28:16–20

### The Great Commission

[16] The eleven disciples traveled to Galilee, to the mountain where Jesus had directed them. [17] When they saw him, they worshiped, but some doubted. [18] Jesus came near and said to them, "All authority has been given to me in heaven and on earth. [19] Go, therefore, and make disciples of all nations, baptizing them in the name of the Father and of the Son and of the Holy Spirit, [20] teaching them to observe everything I have commanded you. And remember, I am with you always, to the end of the age."

## MATTHEW 10:27–42

[27] "What I tell you in the dark, speak in the light. What you hear in a whisper, proclaim on the housetops. [28] Don't fear those who kill the body but are not able to kill the soul; rather, fear him who is able to destroy both soul and body in hell. [29] Aren't two sparrows sold for a penny? Yet not one of them falls to the ground without your Father's consent. [30] But even the hairs of your head have all been counted. [31] So don't be afraid; you are worth more than many sparrows.

### Acknowledging Christ

[32] "Therefore, everyone who will acknowledge me before others, I will also acknowledge him before my Father in heaven. [33] But whoever denies me before others, I will also deny him before my Father in heaven. [34] Don't assume that I came to bring peace on the earth. I did not come to bring peace, but a sword. [35] For I came to turn

> a man against his father,
> a daughter against her mother,
> a daughter-in-law against her mother-in-law;
> [36] and a man's enemies will be
> the members of his household.

[37] The one who loves a father or mother more than me is not worthy of me; the one who loves a son or daughter more than me is not worthy of me. [38] And whoever doesn't take up his cross and follow me is not worthy of me. [39] Anyone who finds his life will lose it, and anyone who loses his life because of me will find it.

### A Cup of Cold Water

[40] "The one who welcomes you welcomes me, and the one who welcomes me welcomes him who sent me. [41] Anyone who welcomes a prophet because he is a prophet will receive a prophet's reward. And anyone who welcomes a righteous person because he's righteous will receive a righteous person's reward. [42] And whoever gives even a cup of cold water to one of these little ones because he is a disciple, truly I tell you, he will never lose his reward."

## ACTS 8:26–38

### The Conversion of the Ethiopian Official

[26] An angel of the Lord spoke to Philip: "Get up and go south to the road that goes down from Jerusalem to Gaza." (This is the desert road.) [27] So he got up and went. There was an Ethiopian man, a eunuch and high official of Candace, queen of the Ethiopians, who was in charge of her entire treasury. He had come to worship in Jerusalem [28] and was sitting in his chariot on his way home, reading the prophet Isaiah aloud.

[29] The Spirit told Philip, "Go and join that chariot."

[30] When Philip ran up to it, he heard him reading the prophet Isaiah, and said, "Do you understand what you're reading?"

[31] "How can I," he said, "unless someone guides me?" So he invited Philip to come up and sit with him. [32] Now the Scripture passage he was reading was this:

> He was led like a sheep to the slaughter,
> and as a lamb is silent before its shearer,
> so he does not open his mouth.
> [33] In his humiliation justice was denied him.
> Who will describe his generation?
> For his life is taken from the earth.

[34] The eunuch said to Philip, "I ask you, who is the prophet saying this about—himself or someone else?" [35] Philip proceeded to tell him the good news about Jesus, beginning with that Scripture.

³⁶ As they were traveling down the road, they came to some water. The eunuch said, "Look, there's water. What would keep me from being baptized?" ³⁸ So he ordered the chariot to stop, and both Philip and the eunuch went down into the water, and he baptized him.

## ROMANS 10:14–17

*Israel's Rejection of the Message*

¹⁴ How, then, can they call on him they have not believed in? And how can they believe without hearing about him? And how can they hear without a preacher? ¹⁵ And how can they preach unless they are sent? As it is written:

How beautiful are the feet of those who bring good news.

¹⁶ But not all obeyed the gospel. For Isaiah says, Lord, who has believed our message? ¹⁷ So faith comes from what is heard, and what is heard comes through the message about Christ.

## 1 CORINTHIANS 1:18–25

*Christ the Power and Wisdom of God*

¹⁸ For the word of the cross is foolishness to those who are perishing, but it is the power of God to us who are being saved. ¹⁹ For it is written,

> I will destroy the wisdom of the wise,
> and I will set aside the intelligence of the intelligent.

²⁰ Where is the one who is wise? Where is the teacher of the law? Where is the debater of this age? Hasn't God made the world's wisdom foolish? ²¹ For since, in God's wisdom, the world did not know God through wisdom, God was pleased to save those who believe through the foolishness of what is preached. ²² For the Jews ask for signs and the Greeks seek wisdom, ²³ but we preach Christ crucified, a stumbling block to the Jews and foolishness to the Gentiles. ²⁴ Yet to those who are called, both Jews and Greeks, Christ is the power of God and the wisdom of God, ²⁵ because God's foolishness is wiser than human wisdom, and God's weakness is stronger than human strength.

## ROMANS 1:16

For I am not ashamed of the gospel, because it is the power of God for salvation to everyone who believes, first to the Jew, and also to the Greek.

SHE READS TRUTH

NOTES

DAY 18

101

"

The Church can have light only as it is full
of the Spirit, and it can be full only as the
members that compose it are filled individually.

—A. W. TOZER

"

# SALT AND LIGHT

*Day 19*

*As the continuation of Christ's ministry on earth, the Church acts as salt and light in a decaying and dark world around us.*

## MATTHEW 5:13–16
*Believers Are Salt and Light*

13 "You are the salt of the earth. But if the salt should lose its taste, how can it be made salty? It's no longer good for anything but to be thrown out and trampled under people's feet.

14 "You are the light of the world. A city situated on a hill cannot be hidden. 15 No one lights a lamp and puts it under a basket, but rather on a lampstand, and it gives light for all who are in the house. 16 In the same way, let your light shine before others, so that they may see your good works and give glory to your Father in heaven."

## GALATIANS 6:10

Therefore, as we have opportunity, let us work for the good of all, especially for those who belong to the household of faith.

## MATTHEW 10:7–8

7 "As you go, proclaim, 'The kingdom of heaven has come near.' 8 Heal the sick, raise the dead, cleanse those with leprosy, drive out demons. Freely you received, freely give."

## LUKE 10:25–37
*The Parable of the Good Samaritan*

25 Then an expert in the law stood up to test him, saying, "Teacher, what must I do to inherit eternal life?"

26 "What is written in the law?" he asked him. "How do you read it?"

27 He answered, "Love the Lord your God with all your heart, with all your soul, with all your strength, and with all your mind," and "your neighbor as yourself."

*"Let your light shine before others."*

---

<sup>28</sup> "You've answered correctly," he told him. "Do this and you will live."

<sup>29</sup> But wanting to justify himself, he asked Jesus, "And who is my neighbor?"

<sup>30</sup> Jesus took up the question and said, "A man was going down from Jerusalem to Jericho and fell into the hands of robbers. They stripped him, beat him up, and fled, leaving him half dead. <sup>31</sup> A priest happened to be going down that road. When he saw him, he passed by on the other side. <sup>32</sup> In the same way, a Levite, when he arrived at the place and saw him, passed by on the other side. <sup>33</sup> But a Samaritan on his journey came up to him, and when he saw the man, he had compassion. <sup>34</sup> He went over to him and bandaged his wounds, pouring on olive oil and wine. Then he put him on his own animal, brought him to an inn, and took care of him. <sup>35</sup> The next day he took out two denarii, gave them to the innkeeper, and said, 'Take care of him. When I come back I'll reimburse you for whatever extra you spend.'

<sup>36</sup> "Which of these three do you think proved to be a neighbor to the man who fell into the hands of the robbers?"

<sup>37</sup> "The one who showed mercy to him," he said.

Then Jesus told him, "Go and do the same."

## MATTHEW 25:31–46
### The Sheep and the Goats

<sup>31</sup> "When the Son of Man comes in his glory, and all the angels with him, then he will sit on his glorious throne. <sup>32</sup> All the nations will be gathered before him, and he will separate them one from another, just as a shepherd separates the sheep from the goats. <sup>33</sup> He will put the sheep on his right and the goats on the left. <sup>34</sup> Then the King will say to those on his right, 'Come, you who are blessed by my Father; inherit the kingdom prepared for you from the foundation of the world.

<sup>35</sup> "'For I was hungry and you gave me something to eat; I was thirsty and you gave me something to drink; I was a stranger and you took me in; <sup>36</sup> I was naked and you clothed me; I was sick and you took care of me; I was in prison and you visited me.'

<sup>37</sup> "Then the righteous will answer him, 'Lord, when did we see you hungry and feed you, or thirsty and give you something to drink? <sup>38</sup> When did we see you a stranger and take you in, or without clothes and clothe you? <sup>39</sup> When did we see you sick, or in prison, and visit you?'

<sup>40</sup> "And the King will answer them, 'Truly I tell you, whatever you did for one of the least of these brothers and sisters of mine, you did for me.'

[41] "Then he will also say to those on the left, 'Depart from me, you who are cursed, into the eternal fire prepared for the devil and his angels! [42] For I was hungry and you gave me nothing to eat; I was thirsty and you gave me nothing to drink; [43] I was a stranger and you didn't take me in; I was naked and you didn't clothe me, sick and in prison and you didn't take care of me.'

[44] "Then they too will answer, 'Lord, when did we see you hungry, or thirsty, or a stranger, or without clothes, or sick, or in prison, and not help you?'

[45] "Then he will answer them, 'Truly I tell you, whatever you did not do for one of the least of these, you did not do for me.'

[46] "And they will go away into eternal punishment, but the righteous into eternal life."

## LUKE 12:33-34

[33] "Sell your possessions and give to the poor. Make money-bags for yourselves that won't grow old, an inexhaustible treasure in heaven, where no thief comes near and no moth destroys. [34] For where your treasure is, there your heart will be also."

## 1 PETER 3:13-17

*Undeserved Suffering*

[13] Who then will harm you if you are devoted to what is good? [14] But even if you should suffer for righteousness, you are blessed. Do not fear them or be intimidated, [15] but in your hearts regard Christ the Lord as holy, ready at any time to give a defense to anyone who asks you for a reason for the hope that is in you. [16] Yet do this with gentleness and reverence, keeping a clear conscience, so that when you are accused, those who disparage your good conduct in Christ will be put to shame. [17] For it is better to suffer for doing good, if that should be God's will, than for doing evil.

## 2 CORINTHIANS 4:1-6

*The Light of the Gospel*

[1] Therefore, since we have this ministry because we were shown mercy, we do not give up. [2] Instead, we have renounced secret and shameful things, not acting deceitfully or distorting the word of God, but commending ourselves before God to everyone's conscience by an open display of the truth. [3] But if our gospel is veiled, it is veiled to those who are perishing. [4] In their case, the god of this age has blinded the minds of the unbelievers to keep them from seeing the light of the gospel of the glory of Christ, who is the image of God. [5] For we are not proclaiming ourselves but Jesus Christ as Lord, and ourselves as your servants for Jesus's sake. [6] For God who said, "Let light shine out of darkness," has shone in our hearts to give the light of the knowledge of God's glory in the face of Jesus Christ.

# Notes

Date

# RESPONSE

*The Church is...*

**A ROYAL PRIESTHOOD**

**THE HOUSEHOLD OF FAITH**

**THE FIRSTFRUITS OF THE NEW CREATION**

**COMMISSIONED BY CHRIST**

**SALT AND LIGHT**

Use these questions as a guide for reflecting on this week's reading. You may not have a response for each one—that's okay!

What truths about the Church stood out to you?

_____

What comforted or encouraged you?

_____

What challenged you?

_____

What questions do you have that you want to explore?

_____

What action might you need to take in response to what you read this week? What is your first step?

_____

1

2

3

4

5

# Pico-de-Guac

PREP TIME: 10 MINUTES
SERVINGS: 3 CUPS

## INGREDIENTS

3 avocados, pitted, peeled, and cut into bite-size pieces

1 large tomato, cored and diced

¼ red onion, finely chopped

Fresh cilantro, chopped, to your liking

Juice of 1 lime (about 2 tablespoons)

Salt, to taste

Tortilla chips

## INSTRUCTIONS

Smash the avocado in a bowl. Then gently fold in the tomatoes and onion. Add the cilantro, lime juice, and salt and stir. Serve with your favorite tortilla chips!

# Grace Day

*Take this day to catch up on your
reading, pray, and rest in the presence
of the Lord.*

BUT TO ALL WHO DID RECEIVE HIM, HE GAVE THEM THE RIGHT TO BE CHILDREN OF GOD, TO THOSE WHO BELIEVE IN HIS NAME, WHO WERE BORN, NOT OF NATURAL DESCENT, OR OF THE WILL OF THE FLESH, OR OF THE WILL OF MAN, BUT OF GOD.

*John 1:12-13*

*Weekly Truth*

*Scripture is God-breathed and true. When we memorize it, we carry the good news of Jesus with us wherever we go.*

*Keep going with your memorization! This week, add verse 4, which highlights the oneness of the Church.*

Therefore I, the prisoner in the Lord, urge you to walk worthy of the calling you have received, with all humility and gentleness, with patience, bearing with one another in love, making every effort to keep the unity of the Spirit through the bond of peace. **There is one body and one Spirit—just as you were called to one hope at your calling**—one Lord, one faith, one baptism, one God and Father of all, who is above all and through all and in all.

EPHESIANS 4:1–6

*See tips for memorizing Scripture on page 182.*

*The Church is*

# MARKED BY BAPTISM

*Jesus, in His own baptism, demonstrates the new life accomplished for us in His death and resurrection. Baptism is an external sign belonging to the people of God.*

# Views of Baptism

At She Reads Truth, our primary goal is to invite and equip you to read the Bible. Today's readings are on the importance of baptism. Across the spectrum of Christianity, baptism marks a person's entry into the community of faith and demonstrates a connection with Jesus. Interpretations on the further purposes, meaning, and practice of baptism differ among traditions that faithfully follow Jesus and uphold the authority of Scripture. Below is a summary of three such perspectives on baptism.

---

**INFANT BAPTISM**

In some traditions, parents are encouraged to have their young children baptized. This baptism ritual is a sign and symbol of God's promises to His people, the Church. In this view, baptism is a replacement for the symbol of circumcision in the Abrahamic covenant.

---

**BELIEVER'S BAPTISM**

In other traditions, baptism occurs after an individual's confession of faith. This baptism ritual is an outward sign and symbol of a personal, inward experience of belief in Jesus. In this view, it is belief, or "circumcision of the heart," that replaces the symbol of circumcision in the Abrahamic covenant.

---

**DUAL-PRACTICE BAPTISM**

Some churches permit both views to be practiced side by side as a means of honoring what is represented in each.

**SCRIPTURES ABOUT BAPTISM**

*Matthew 3:13–17; 28:19; John 3:3–6; Acts 2:14–41; 8:12, 26–39; 16:25–34; Romans 6:1–11; 1 Corinthians 12:13; Galatians 3:27; Ephesians 4:1–6; 1 Peter 3:18–22*

## MATTHEW 3:13–17
*The Baptism of Jesus*

13 Then Jesus came from Galilee to John at the Jordan, to be baptized by him. 14 But John tried to stop him, saying, "I need to be baptized by you, and yet you come to me?"

15 Jesus answered him, "Allow it for now, because this is the way for us to fulfill all righteousness." Then John allowed him to be baptized.

16 When Jesus was baptized, he went up immediately from the water. The heavens suddenly opened for him, and he saw the Spirit of God descending like a dove and coming down on him. 17 And a voice from heaven said, "This is my beloved Son, with whom I am well-pleased."

## JOHN 3:3–6
3 Jesus replied, "Truly I tell you, unless someone is born again, he cannot see the kingdom of God."

4 "How can anyone be born when he is old?" Nicodemus asked him. "Can he enter his mother's womb a second time and be born?"

5 Jesus answered, "Truly I tell you, unless someone is born of water and the Spirit, he cannot enter the kingdom of God. 6 Whatever is born of the flesh is flesh, and whatever is born of the Spirit is spirit."

## ROMANS 6:1–11
*The New Life in Christ*

1 What should we say then? Should we continue in sin so that grace may multiply? 2 Absolutely not! How can we who died to sin still live in it?

3 Or are you unaware that all of us who were baptized into Christ Jesus were baptized into his death?

4 Therefore we were buried with him by baptism into death, in order that, just as Christ was raised from the dead by the glory of the Father, so we too may walk in newness of life. 5 For if we have been united with him in the likeness of his death, we will certainly also be in the likeness of his resurrection. 6 For we know that our old self was crucified with him so that the body ruled by sin might be rendered powerless so that we may no longer be enslaved to sin, 7 since a person who has died is freed from sin. 8 Now if we died with Christ, we believe that we will also live with him, 9 because we know that Christ, having been raised from the dead, will not die again. Death no longer rules over him. 10 For the death he died, he died to sin once for all time; but the life he lives, he lives to God. 11 So, you too consider yourselves dead to sin and alive to God in Christ Jesus.

## 1 PETER 3:18–22
18 For Christ also suffered for sins once for all, the righteous for the unrighteous, that he might bring you to God. He was put to death in the flesh but made alive by the Spirit, 19 in which he also went and made proclamation to the spirits in prison 20 who in the past were disobedient, when God patiently waited in the days of Noah while the ark was being prepared. In it a few—that is, eight people—were saved through water. 21 Baptism, which corresponds to this, now saves you (not as the removal of dirt from the body, but the pledge of a good conscience toward God) through the resurrection of Jesus Christ, 22 who has gone into heaven and is at the right hand of God with angels, authorities, and powers subject to him.

## GALATIANS 3:27
For those of you who were baptized into Christ have been clothed with Christ.

THE CHURCH IS

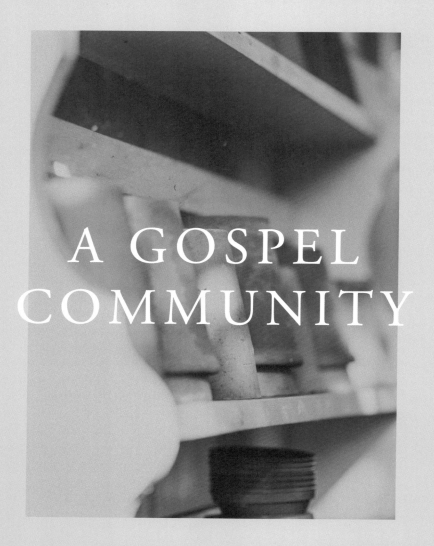

# A GOSPEL COMMUNITY

*As a community of people shaped by the gospel, the Church is called to love and serve one another, meeting each other's needs and encouraging one another in godliness.*

*Day 23*

*"By this everyone will know
that you are my disciples,
if you love one another."*

---

## JOHN 13:34–35

34 "I give you a new command: Love one another. Just as I have loved you, you are also to love one another. 35 By this everyone will know that you are my disciples, if you love one another."

## ACTS 2:42–47
*A Generous and Growing Church*

42 They devoted themselves to the apostles' teaching, to the fellowship, to the breaking of bread, and to prayer.

43 Everyone was filled with awe, and many wonders and signs were being performed through the apostles. 44 Now all the believers were together and held all things in common. 45 They sold their possessions and property and distributed the proceeds to all, as any had need. 46 Every day they devoted themselves to meeting together in the temple, and broke bread from house to house. They ate their food with joyful and sincere hearts, 47 praising God and enjoying the favor of all the people. Every day the Lord added to their number those who were being saved.

## ACTS 4:32–35
*All Things in Common*

32 Now the entire group of those who believed were of one heart and mind, and no one claimed that any of his possessions was his own, but instead they held everything in common. 33 With great power the apostles were giving testimony to the resurrection of the Lord Jesus, and great grace was on all of them. 34 For there was not a needy person among them because all those who owned lands or houses sold them, brought the proceeds of what was sold, 35 and laid them at the apostles' feet. This was then distributed to each person as any had need.

## JAMES 1:27

Pure and undefiled religion before God the Father is this: to look after orphans and widows in their distress and to keep oneself unstained from the world.

## JAMES 2:14–19, 26
*Faith and Works*

14 What good is it, my brothers and sisters, if someone claims to have faith but does not have works? Can such faith save him?

15 If a brother or sister is without clothes and lacks daily food 16 and one of you says to them, "Go in peace, stay warm, and be well fed," but you don't give them what the body needs, what good is it? 17 In the same way faith, if it does not have works, is dead by itself.

[18] But someone will say, "You have faith, and I have works." Show me your faith without works, and I will show you faith by my works. [19] You believe that God is one. Good! Even the demons believe—and they shudder.

...

[26] For just as the body without the spirit is dead, so also faith without works is dead.

## ROMANS 12:13

Share with the saints in their needs; pursue hospitality.

## 1 JOHN 3:11–18

*Love in Action*

[11] For this is the message you have heard from the beginning: We should love one another, [12] unlike Cain, who was of the evil one and murdered his brother. And why did he murder him? Because his deeds were evil, and his brother's were righteous.

[13] Do not be surprised, brothers and sisters, if the world hates you. [14] We know that we have passed from death to life because we love our brothers and sisters. The one who does not love remains in death. [15] Everyone who hates his brother or sister is a murderer, and you know that no murderer has eternal life residing in him.

[16] This is how we have come to know love: He laid down his life for us. We should also lay down our lives for our brothers and sisters.

[17] If anyone has this world's goods and sees a fellow believer in need but withholds compassion from him—how does God's love reside in him? [18] Little children, let us not love in word or speech, but in action and in truth.

## HEBREWS 10:24–25

[24] And let us consider one another in order to provoke love and good works, [25] not neglecting to gather together, as some are in the habit of doing, but encouraging each other, and all the more as you see the day approaching.

## GALATIANS 5:13–24

[13] For you were called to be free, brothers and sisters; only don't use this freedom as an opportunity for the flesh, but serve one another through love. [14] For the whole law is fulfilled in one statement: Love your neighbor as yourself. [15] But if you bite and devour one another, watch out, or you will be consumed by one another.

[16] I say, then, walk by the Spirit and you will certainly not carry out the desire of the flesh. [17] For the flesh desires what is against the Spirit, and the Spirit desires what is against the flesh; these are opposed to each other, so that you don't do what you want. [18] But if you are led by the Spirit, you are not under the law.

[19] Now the works of the flesh are obvious: sexual immorality, moral impurity, promiscuity, [20] idolatry, sorcery, hatreds, strife, jealousy, outbursts of anger, selfish ambitions, dissensions, factions, [21] envy, drunkenness, carousing, and anything similar. I am warning you about these things—as I warned you before—that those who practice such things will not inherit the kingdom of God.

[22] But the fruit of the Spirit is love, joy, peace, patience, kindness, goodness, faithfulness, [23] gentleness, and self-control. The law is not against such things. [24] Now those who belong to Christ Jesus have crucified the flesh with its passions and desires.

"

It is grace, nothing but grace, that we
are allowed to live in community with
Christian brethren.

—DIETRICH BONHOEFFER

"

*The Church is*

# A PEOPLE OF REMEMBRANCE

---

*The Lord's Supper (also known as the Eucharist or Communion) was established by Jesus when He observed the Passover meal with His disciples. The Lord's Supper proclaims the gospel to ourselves and to one another.*

[47] "Truly I tell you, anyone who believes has eternal life. [48] I am the bread of life. [49] Your ancestors ate the manna in the wilderness, and they died. [50] This is the bread that comes down from heaven so that anyone may eat of it and not die. [51] I am the living bread that came down from heaven. If anyone eats of this bread he will live forever. The bread that I will give for the life of the world is my flesh."

[52] At that, the Jews argued among themselves, "How can this man give us his flesh to eat?"

[53] So Jesus said to them, "Truly I tell you, unless you eat the flesh of the Son of Man and drink his blood, you do not have life in yourselves. [54] The one who eats my flesh and drinks my blood has eternal life, and I will raise him up on the last day, [55] because my flesh is true food and my blood is true drink. [56] The one who eats my flesh and drinks my blood remains in me, and I in him. [57] Just as the living Father sent me and I live because of the Father, so the one who feeds on me will live because of me. [58] This is the bread that came down from heaven; it is not like the manna your ancestors ate—and they died. The one who eats this bread will live forever."

## MATTHEW 26:26–29

*The First Lord's Supper*

[26] As they were eating, Jesus took bread, blessed and broke it, gave it to the disciples, and said, "Take and eat it; this is my body." [27] Then he took a cup, and after giving thanks, he gave it to them and said, "Drink from it, all of you. [28] For this is my blood of the covenant, which is poured out for many for the forgiveness of sins. [29] But I tell you, I will not drink from this fruit of the vine from now on until that day when I drink it new with you in my Father's kingdom."

## EXODUS 12:1–3, 7–13, 21–28

*Instructions for the Passover*

[1] The Lord said to Moses and Aaron in the land of Egypt, [2] "This month is to be the beginning of months for you; it is the first month of your year. [3] Tell the whole community of Israel that on the tenth day of this month they must each select an animal of the flock according to their fathers' families, one animal per family."

…

[7] "They must take some of the blood and put it on the two doorposts and the lintel of the houses where they eat them. [8] They are to eat the meat that night; they should eat it, roasted over the fire along with unleavened bread and bitter herbs. [9] Do not eat any of it raw or cooked in boiling water, but only roasted over fire—its head as well as its legs and inner organs. [10] You must not leave any of it until morning; any part of it left until morning you must burn. [11] Here is how you must eat it: You must be dressed for travel, your sandals on your feet, and your staff in your hand. You are to eat it in a hurry; it is the Lord's Passover.

[12] "I will pass through the land of Egypt on that night and strike every firstborn male in the land of Egypt, both people and animals. I am the Lord; I will execute judgments against all the gods of Egypt. [13] The blood on the houses where you are staying will be a distinguishing mark for you; when I see the blood, I will pass over you. No plague will be among you to destroy you when I strike the land of Egypt."

…

[21] Then Moses summoned all the elders of Israel and said to them, "Go, select an animal from the flock according to your families, and slaughter the Passover animal. [22] Take a cluster of hyssop, dip it in the blood that is in the basin, and brush the lintel and the two doorposts with some of the blood in the basin. None of you may go out the door of his house until morning. [23] When the Lord passes through to strike Egypt and sees the blood on the lintel and the two doorposts, he will pass over the door and not let the destroyer enter your houses to strike you.

[24] "Keep this command permanently as a statute for you and your descendants. [25] When you enter the land that the Lord will give you as he promised, you are to observe this ceremony. [26] When your children ask you, 'What does this ceremony mean to you?' [27] you are to reply, 'It is the Passover sacrifice to the Lord, for he passed over the houses of the Israelites in Egypt when he struck the Egyptians, and he spared our homes.'" So the people knelt low and worshiped. [28] Then the Israelites went and did this; they did just as the Lord had commanded Moses and Aaron.

[16] The cup of blessing that we bless, is it not a sharing in the blood of Christ? The bread that we break, is it not a sharing in the body of Christ? [17] Because there is one bread, we who are many are one body, since all of us share the one bread.

## 1 CORINTHIANS 11:17-29

### The Lord's Supper

[17] Now in giving this instruction I do not praise you, since you come together not for the better but for the worse. [18] For to begin with, I hear that when you come together as a church there are divisions among you, and in part I believe it. [19] Indeed, it is necessary that there be factions among you, so that those who are approved may be recognized among you. [20] When you come together, then, it is not to eat the Lord's Supper. [21] For at the meal, each one eats his own supper. So one person is hungry while another gets drunk! [22] Don't you have homes in which to eat and drink? Or do you despise the church of God and humiliate those who have nothing? What should I say to you? Should I praise you? I do not praise you in this matter!

[23] For I received from the Lord what I also passed on to you: On the night when he was betrayed, the Lord Jesus took bread, [24] and when he had given thanks, broke it, and said,

> "This is my body, which is for you. Do this in remembrance of me."

[25] In the same way also he took the cup, after supper, and said, "This cup is the new covenant in my blood. Do this, as often as you drink it, in remembrance of me." [26] For as often as you eat this bread and drink the cup, you proclaim the Lord's death until he comes.

### Self-Examination

[27] So, then, whoever eats the bread or drinks the cup of the Lord in an unworthy manner will be guilty of sin against the body and blood of the Lord. [28] Let a person examine himself; in this way let him eat the bread and drink from the cup. [29] For whoever eats and drinks without recognizing the body, eats and drinks judgment on himself.

## PSALM 34:8

Taste and see that the LORD is good.
How happy is the person who takes refuge in him!

# Notes

_____

*Date*

THE CHURCH IS

# PROCLAIMING THE WORD

*The Church is shaped, convicted, and encouraged by the teaching and sharing of God's Word.*

*Day 25*

[16] He came to Nazareth, where he had been brought up. As usual, he entered the synagogue on the Sabbath day and stood up to read. [17] The scroll of the prophet Isaiah was given to him, and unrolling the scroll, he found the place where it was written:

> [18] The Spirit of the Lord is on me,
> because he has anointed me
> to preach good news to the poor.
> He has sent me
> to proclaim release to the captives
> and recovery of sight to the blind,
> to set free the oppressed,
> [19] to proclaim the year of the Lord's favor.

[20] He then rolled up the scroll, gave it back to the attendant, and sat down. And the eyes of everyone in the synagogue were fixed on him. [21] He began by saying to them, "Today as you listen, this Scripture has been fulfilled."

## LUKE 24:13-35

*The Emmaus Disciples*

[13] Now that same day two of them were on their way to a village called Emmaus, which was about seven miles from Jerusalem. [14] Together they were discussing everything that had taken place. [15] And while they were discussing and arguing, Jesus himself came near and began to walk along with them. [16] But they were prevented from recognizing him. [17] Then he asked them, "What is this dispute that you're having with each other as you are walking?" And they stopped walking and looked discouraged.

[18] The one named Cleopas answered him, "Are you the only visitor in Jerusalem who doesn't know the things that happened there in these days?"

[19] "What things?" he asked them.

So they said to him, "The things concerning Jesus of Nazareth, who was a prophet powerful in action and speech before God and all the people, [20] and how our chief priests and leaders handed him over to be sentenced to death, and they crucified him. [21] But we were hoping that he was the one who was about to redeem Israel. Besides all this, it's the third day since these things happened. [22] Moreover, some women from our group astounded us. They arrived early at the tomb, [23] and when they didn't find his body, they came and reported that they had seen a vision of angels who said he was alive. [24] Some of those who were with us went to the tomb and found it just as the women had said, but they didn't see him."

25 He said to them, "How foolish you are, and how slow to believe all that the prophets have spoken! 26 Wasn't it necessary for the Messiah to suffer these things and enter into his glory?" 27 Then beginning with Moses and all the Prophets, he interpreted for them the things concerning himself in all the Scriptures.

28 They came near the village where they were going, and he gave the impression that he was going farther. 29 But they urged him, "Stay with us, because it's almost evening, and now the day is almost over." So he went in to stay with them.

30 It was as he reclined at the table with them that he took the bread, blessed and broke it, and gave it to them. 31 Then their eyes were opened, and they recognized him, but he disappeared from their sight. 32 They said to each other, "Weren't our hearts burning within us while he was talking with us on the road and explaining the Scriptures to us?" 33 That very hour they got up and returned to Jerusalem. They found the Eleven and those with them gathered together, 34 who said, "The Lord has truly been raised and has appeared to Simon!" 35 Then they began to describe what had happened on the road and how he was made known to them in the breaking of the bread.

## 1 TIMOTHY 4:13

Until I come, give your attention to public reading, exhortation, and teaching.

## 2 TIMOTHY 3:16–17

16 All Scripture is inspired by God and is profitable for teaching, for rebuking, for correcting, for training in righteousness, 17 so that the man of God may be complete, equipped for every good work.

## COLOSSIANS 3:16

## Let the word of Christ dwell richly among you,

in all wisdom teaching and admonishing one another through psalms, hymns, and spiritual songs, singing to God with gratitude in your hearts.

## HEBREWS 4:12–13

12 For the word of God is living and effective and sharper than any double-edged sword, penetrating as far as the separation of soul and spirit, joints and marrow. It is able to judge the thoughts and intentions of the heart. 13 No creature is hidden from him, but all things are naked and exposed to the eyes of him to whom we must give an account.

## 1 THESSALONIANS 5:27

I charge you by the Lord that this letter be read to all the brothers and sisters.

## COLOSSIANS 4:16

After this letter has been read at your gathering, have it read also in the church of the Laodiceans; and see that you also read the letter from Laodicea.

## PSALM 119:97–105

[97] How I love your instruction!
It is my meditation all day long.
[98] Your command makes me wiser than my enemies,
for it is always with me.
[99] I have more insight than all my teachers
because your decrees are my meditation.
[100] I understand more than the elders
because I obey your precepts.
[101] I have kept my feet from every evil path
to follow your word.
[102] I have not turned from your judgments,
for you yourself have instructed me.
[103] How sweet your word is to my taste—
sweeter than honey in my mouth.
[104] I gain understanding from your precepts;
therefore I hate every false way.

[105] Your word is a lamp for my feet
and a light on my path.

# CORPORATE WORSHIP

Scripture calls us to worship God with other believers. While worship styles and expressions vary across denominations and traditions, the Church gathers together to worship one God—to remember what He has done, is doing, and will do. Here is a look at some of what the Bible says about gathering in worship.

## Corporate Worship in the Old Testament

*Qahal* is the Hebrew word often used for "assembly" in the Old Testament. It refers to a group of people coming together for a particular purpose, typically worship or war.

JOS 18:1; 1KG 8:1–2; 2CH 20:26

God instructed the Israelites to gather together at specific times to remember how God brought them out of Egypt and to thank Him for all He had done.

LV 23

God's people came together in worship to dedicate themselves to the Lord and to their covenant with Him.

DT 29:1–32:47; 2KG 23:1–3; NEH 8–10

## Corporate Worship in the New Testament

*Ekklesia* is the word used for *qahal* in the Greek translation of the Old Testament (known as the Septuagint). It was later used in the New Testament to describe both the Church in the universal sense and the church within a specific region.

AC 5:11; 8:1; 9:31; RM 16:5; RV 1:4

While teaching His disciples how to confront a sinful brother, Jesus promised that when two or three gather in His name, He will be there with them.

MT 18:15–20

Corporate worship in the early Church typically took place in people's homes and involved singing, teaching, eating, participating in the Lord's Supper, praying for one another, and responding to the needs of the community. The New Testament includes letters to different churches, encouraging them to continue gathering together and reminding them of their identity as God's people.

AC 2:42–45; RM 16:23; 1CO 11:23–26; 14:26; JMS 5:16

# PRESERVING THE MESSAGE

*Day 26*

*The Church is called to faithfully teach the gospel of Jesus as presented through Scripture, passed down from eyewitnesses and the apostles. We are to guard against false teachings and ideologies that alter or distract from the good news.*

## ACTS 15:1–35

### Dispute in Antioch

¹ Some men came down from Judea and began to teach the brothers, "Unless you are circumcised according to the custom prescribed by Moses, you cannot be saved." ² After Paul and Barnabas had engaged them in serious argument and debate, Paul and Barnabas and some others were appointed to go up to the apostles and elders in Jerusalem about this issue. ³ When they had been sent on their way by the church, they passed through both Phoenicia and Samaria, describing in detail the conversion of the Gentiles, and they brought great joy to all the brothers and sisters.

⁴ When they arrived at Jerusalem, they were welcomed by the church, the apostles, and the elders, and they reported all that God had done with them. ⁵ But some of the believers who belonged to the party of the Pharisees stood up and said, "It is necessary to circumcise them and to command them to keep the law of Moses."

### The Jerusalem Council

⁶ The apostles and the elders gathered to consider this matter. ⁷ After there had been much debate, Peter stood up and said to them, "Brothers, you are aware that in the early days God made a choice among you, that by my mouth the Gentiles would hear the gospel message and believe. ⁸ And God, who knows the heart, bore witness to them by giving them the Holy Spirit, just as he also did to us. ⁹ He made no distinction between us and them, cleansing their hearts by faith. ¹⁰ Now then, why are you testing God by putting a yoke on the disciples' necks that neither our ancestors nor we have been able to bear? ¹¹ On the contrary, we believe that we are saved through the grace of the Lord Jesus in the same way they are."

¹² The whole assembly became silent and listened to Barnabas and Paul describe all the signs and wonders God had done through them among the Gentiles. ¹³ After they

stopped speaking, James responded, "Brothers, listen to me. [14] Simeon has reported how God first intervened to take from the Gentiles a people for his name. [15] And the words of the prophets agree with this, as it is written:

[16] After these things I will return
and rebuild David's fallen tent.
I will rebuild its ruins
and set it up again,
[17] so that the rest of humanity
may seek the Lord—
even all the Gentiles
who are called by my name—
declares the Lord
who makes these things [18] known from long ago.

[19] Therefore, in my judgment, we should not cause difficulties for those among the Gentiles who turn to God, [20] but instead we should write to them to abstain from things polluted by idols, from sexual immorality, from eating anything that has been strangled, and from blood. [21] For since ancient times, Moses has had those who proclaim him in every city, and every Sabbath day he is read aloud in the synagogues."

### The Letter to the Gentile Believers

[22] Then the apostles and the elders, with the whole church, decided to select men who were among them and to send them to Antioch with Paul and Barnabas: Judas, called Barsabbas, and Silas, both leading men among the brothers. [23] They wrote:

"From the apostles and the elders, your brothers,

To the brothers and sisters among the Gentiles in Antioch, Syria, and Cilicia:

Greetings.

[24] Since we have heard that some without our authorization went out from us and troubled you with their words and unsettled your hearts, [25] we have unanimously decided to select men and send them to you along with our dearly loved Barnabas and Paul, [26] who have risked their lives for the name of our Lord Jesus Christ. [27] Therefore we have

sent Judas and Silas, who will personally report the same things by word of mouth. [28] For it was the Holy Spirit's decision—and ours—not to place further burdens on you beyond these requirements: [29] that you abstain from food offered to idols, from blood, from eating anything that has been strangled, and from sexual immorality. You will do well if you keep yourselves from these things.

Farewell."

### The Outcome of the Jerusalem Letter

[30] So they were sent off and went down to Antioch, and after gathering the assembly, they delivered the letter. [31] When they read it, they rejoiced because of its encouragement. [32] Both Judas and Silas, who were also prophets themselves, encouraged the brothers and sisters and strengthened them with a long message. [33] After spending some time there, they were sent back in peace by the brothers and sisters to those who had sent them. [35] But Paul and Barnabas, along with many others, remained in Antioch, teaching and proclaiming the word of the Lord.

## 1 CORINTHIANS 15:1–8
### Resurrection Essential to the Gospel

[1] Now I want to make clear for you, brothers and sisters, the gospel I preached to you, which you received, on which you have taken your stand [2] and by which you are being saved, if you hold to the message I preached to you—unless you believed in vain. [3] For I passed on to you as most important what I also received: that Christ died for our sins according to the Scriptures, [4] that he was buried, that he was raised on the third day according to the Scriptures, [5] and that he appeared to Cephas, then to the Twelve. [6] Then he appeared to over five hundred brothers and sisters at one time; most of them are still alive, but some have fallen asleep. [7] Then he appeared to James, then to all the apostles. [8] Last of all, as to one born at the wrong time, he also appeared to me.

## LUKE 1:1–4
### The Dedication to Theophilus

[1] Many have undertaken to compile a narrative about the events that have been fulfilled among us, [2] just as the original

eyewitnesses and servants of the word handed them down to us. ³ So it also seemed good to me, since I have carefully investigated everything from the very first, to write to you in an orderly sequence, most honorable Theophilus, ⁴ so that you may know the certainty of the things about which you have been instructed.

## HEBREWS 13:8–9

⁸ Jesus Christ is the same yesterday, today, and forever. ⁹ Don't be led astray by various kinds of strange teachings; for it is good for the heart to be established by grace and not by food regulations, since those who observe them have not benefited.

## 1 CORINTHIANS 11:2

Now I praise you because you remember me in everything and hold fast to the traditions just as I delivered them to you.

## 1 THESSALONIANS 2:13

This is why we constantly thank God, because when you received the word of God that you heard from us, you welcomed it not as a human message, but as it truly is, the word of God, which also works effectively in you who believe.

## 2 THESSALONIANS 2:15

So then, brothers and sisters, stand firm and hold to the traditions you were taught, whether by what we said or what we wrote.

## 2 TIMOTHY 1:13–14

*Be Loyal to the Faith*

¹³ Hold on to the pattern of sound teaching that you have heard from me,

in the faith and love that are in Christ Jesus. ¹⁴ Guard the good deposit through the Holy Spirit who lives in us.

## 2 TIMOTHY 2:2

What you have heard from me in the presence of many witnesses, commit to faithful men who will be able to teach others also.

## 2 TIMOTHY 4:3

For the time will come when people will not tolerate sound doctrine, but according to their own desires, will multiply teachers for themselves because they have an itch to hear what they want to hear.

# Notes

_____

*Date*

# RESPONSE

*The Church is...*

MARKED BY BAPTISM

A GOSPEL COMMUNITY

A PEOPLE OF REMEMBRANCE

PROCLAIMING THE WORD

PRESERVING THE MESSAGE

Use these questions as a guide for reflecting on this week's reading. You may not have a response for each one—that's okay!

What truths about the Church stood out to you?

_____

What comforted or encouraged you?

_____

What challenged you?

_____

What questions do you have that you want to explore?

_____

What action might you need to take in response to what you read this week? What is your first step?

_____

1

2

3

4

5

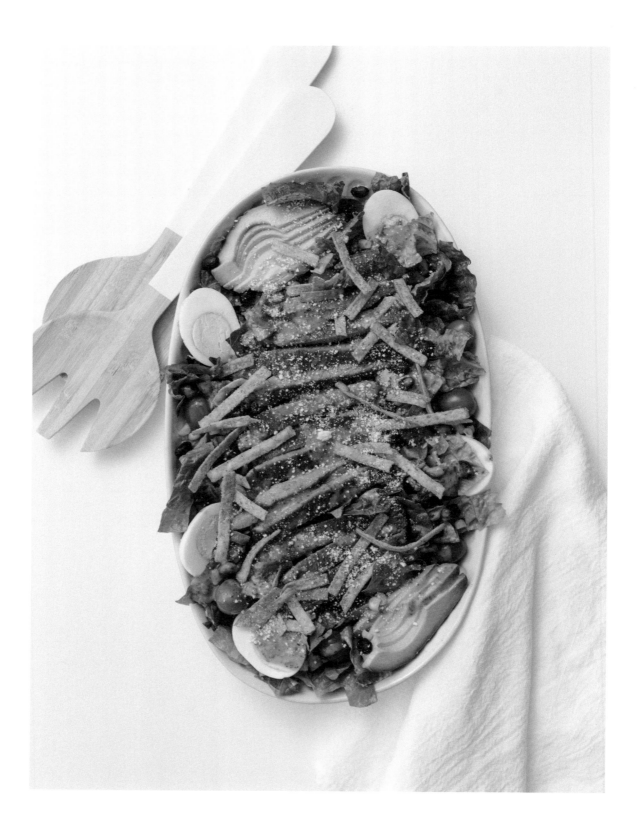

# Steak Salad

PREP TIME: 1 HOUR
COOK TIME: 20 MINUTES
SERVES: 6–8

---

## INGREDIENTS

*Steak*

1 pound flank steak

Olive oil, to coat steak

1 (1-ounce) taco seasoning packet

*Tortilla Strips*

8 tortillas, cut into thin, small strips

1 tablespoon taco seasoning

1 tablespoon olive oil

*Dressing*

½ cup apple cider vinegar

3 tablespoons ume plum vinegar
(or red wine wine vinegar)

2 cups fresh cilantro leaves

¼ to ½ avocado

2 to 4 cloves garlic, peeled and minced

½ teaspoon pepper

¾ cups olive oil, plus more to taste

*Salad*

2 heads romaine lettuce, cut into bite-size pieces

1 avocado, pitted, peeled, and sliced

1 cup black beans, cooked

1 cup cherry tomatoes

1 cup fresh cilantro leaves, chopped

1 cup canned corn, drained

3 hard-boiled eggs, sliced

1 cup cojita cheese, crumbled

## INSTRUCTIONS

*To marinate the steak*

Rub the steak with a drizzle of olive oil and taco seasoning and marinate in the fridge for at least 1 hour.

*For the tortilla strips*

Preheat the oven to 350°F. Line a baking sheet with parchment paper.

In a bowl, toss the tortilla strips with the taco seasoning and olive oil, making sure all the strips are well coated. Spread on the baking sheet and bake for 10 to 15 minutes, until crisp. Keep an eye on them because they can burn easily! Set aside. (You can make these a few days ahead.)

*For the dressing*

In a food processor, combine the cider vinegar, plum vinegar, cilantro, avocado, garlic, and pepper. Blend. With the processor running, slowly add the olive oil until well blended. If it's too vinegary for you, add more olive oil.

*For the salad*

Preheat a grill to high heat. Cook the steak, turning once or twice, to desired doneness, and let it rest for 10 minutes. Slice the steak into long, thin pieces.

Place the lettuce in a large bowl and arrange the steak and all remaining ingredients on top. Pour dressing evenly over the salad, or serve on the side.

# Grace Day

*Take this day to catch up on your reading, pray, and rest in the presence of the Lord.*

# LET THE WORD OF CHRIST DWELL RICHLY AMONG YOU.

*Colossians 3:16*

DAY 28

*Weekly Truth*

*Scripture is God-breathed and true. When we memorize it, we carry the good news of Jesus with us wherever we go.*

*This week we will add our final verses, 5 and 6, to our memorization of Paul's encouragement about the unity that characterizes the body of Christ.*

Therefore I, the prisoner in the Lord, urge you to walk worthy of the calling you have received, with all humility and gentleness, with patience, bearing with one another in love, making every effort to keep the unity of the Spirit through the bond of peace. There is one body and one Spirit—just as you were called to one hope at your calling—one Lord, one faith, one baptism, one God and Father of all, who is above all and through all and in all.

EPHESIANS 4:1–6

*See tips for memorizing Scripture on page 182.*

The Church is

# CALLED
# TO PRAYER

*Just as the Spirit intercedes on our behalf, the Church is to pray with confidence
for our own needs, as well as the needs of other believers and the world.*

## 1 TIMOTHY 2:1–4

*Instructions on Prayer*

[1] First of all, then, I urge that petitions, prayers, intercessions, and thanksgivings be made for everyone, [2] for kings and all those who are in authority, so that we may lead a tranquil and quiet life in all godliness and dignity. [3] This is good, and it pleases God our Savior, [4] who wants everyone to be saved and to come to the knowledge of the truth.

## MATTHEW 6:5–15

*How to Pray*

[5] "Whenever you pray, you must not be like the hypocrites, because they love to pray standing in the synagogues and on the street corners to be seen by people. Truly I tell you, they have their reward. [6] But when you pray, go into your private room, shut your door, and pray to your Father who is in secret. And your Father who sees in secret will reward you. [7] When you pray, don't babble like the Gentiles, since they imagine they'll be heard for their many words. [8] Don't be like them, because your Father knows the things you need before you ask him.

*The Lord's Prayer*

[9] "Therefore, you should pray like this:

Our Father in heaven,
your name be honored as holy.
[10] Your kingdom come.
Your will be done
on earth as it is in heaven.
[11] Give us today our daily bread.
[12] And forgive us our debts,
as we also have forgiven our debtors.
[13] And do not bring us into temptation,
but deliver us from the evil one.

[14] "For if you forgive others their offenses, your heavenly Father will forgive you as well. [15] But if you don't forgive others, your Father will not forgive your offenses."

## LUKE 18:1–8

*The Parable of the Persistent Widow*

[1] Now he told them a parable on the need for them to pray always and not give up. [2] "There was a judge in a certain town who didn't fear God or respect people. [3] And a widow in that town kept coming to him, saying, 'Give me justice against my adversary.'

# Pray at all times in the Spirit with every prayer and request.

---

⁴ "For a while he was unwilling, but later he said to himself, 'Even though I don't fear God or respect people, ⁵ yet because this widow keeps pestering me, I will give her justice, so that she doesn't wear me out by her persistent coming.'"

⁶ Then the Lord said, "Listen to what the unjust judge says. ⁷ Will not God grant justice to his elect who cry out to him day and night? Will he delay helping them? ⁸ I tell you that he will swiftly grant them justice. Nevertheless, when the Son of Man comes, will he find faith on earth?"

## EPHESIANS 6:18
Pray at all times in the Spirit with every prayer and request, and stay alert with all perseverance and intercession for all the saints.

## 1 THESSALONIANS 5:16–18
¹⁶ Rejoice always, ¹⁷ pray constantly, ¹⁸ give thanks in everything; for this is God's will for you in Christ Jesus.

## PHILIPPIANS 4:4–7
⁴ Rejoice in the Lord always. I will say it again: Rejoice! ⁵ Let your graciousness be known to everyone. The Lord is near. ⁶ Don't worry about anything, but in everything, through prayer and petition with thanksgiving, present your requests to God. ⁷ And the peace of God, which surpasses all understanding, will guard your hearts and minds in Christ Jesus.

## 1 JOHN 5:14–15
*Effective Prayer*

¹⁴ This is the confidence we have before him: If we ask anything according to his will, he hears us. ¹⁵ And if we know that he hears whatever we ask, we know that we have what we have asked of him.

## HEBREWS 4:14–16
*Our Great High Priest*

¹⁴ Therefore, since we have a great high priest who has passed through the heavens—Jesus the Son of God—let us hold fast to our confession. ¹⁵ For we do not have a high priest who is unable to sympathize with our weaknesses, but one who has been tempted in every way as we are, yet without sin. ¹⁶ Therefore, let us approach the throne of grace with boldness, so that we may receive mercy and find grace to help us in time of need.

## ROMANS 8:26–27
²⁶ In the same way the Spirit also helps us in our weakness, because we do not know what to pray for as we should, but the Spirit himself intercedes for us with inexpressible groanings. ²⁷ And he who searches our hearts knows the mind of the Spirit, because he intercedes for the saints according to the will of God.

*Notes*

_Date_

# A PEOPLE IN PROGRESS

*Day 30*

*As a people still being transformed into the likeness of Christ, the Church has fallen short and will continue to. Until Christ's return, the Church is called to both individual and corporate repentance, knowing that Christ is faithful to forgive, sustain, and perfect His people.*

## JAMES 4:1–8, 11–12
*Proud or Humble*

¹ What is the source of wars and fights among you? Don't they come from your passions that wage war within you? ² You desire and do not have. You murder and covet and cannot obtain. You fight and wage war. You do not have because you do not ask. ³ You ask and don't receive because you ask with wrong motives, so that you may spend it on your pleasures.

⁴ You adulterous people! Don't you know that friendship with the world is hostility toward God?

So whoever wants to be the friend of the world becomes the enemy of God.

⁵ Or do you think it's without reason that the Scripture says: The spirit he made to dwell in us envies intensely?

⁶ But he gives greater grace. Therefore he says:

God resists the proud
but gives grace to the humble.

⁷ Therefore, submit to God. Resist the devil, and he will flee from you. ⁸ Draw near to God, and he will draw near to you. Cleanse your hands, sinners, and purify your hearts, you double-minded.

…

[11] Don't criticize one another, brothers and sisters. Anyone who defames or judges a fellow believer defames and judges the law. If you judge the law, you are not a doer of the law but a judge. [12] There is one lawgiver and judge who is able to save and to destroy. But who are you to judge your neighbor?

## GALATIANS 2:11–16
### Freedom from the Law

[11] But when Cephas came to Antioch, I opposed him to his face because he stood condemned. [12] For he regularly ate with the Gentiles before certain men came from James. However, when they came, he withdrew and separated himself, because he feared those from the circumcision party. [13] Then the rest of the Jews joined his hypocrisy, so that even Barnabas was led astray by their hypocrisy. [14] But when I saw that they were deviating from the truth of the gospel, I told Cephas in front of everyone, "If you, who are a Jew, live like a Gentile and not like a Jew, how can you compel Gentiles to live like Jews?"

[15] We are Jews by birth and not "Gentile sinners," [16] and yet because we know that a person is not justified by the works of the law but by faith in Jesus Christ, even we ourselves have believed in Christ Jesus. This was so that we might be justified by faith in Christ and not by the works of the law, because by the works of the law no human being will be justified.

## REVELATION 2:1–5
### The Letter to Ephesus

[1] "Write to the angel of the church in Ephesus: Thus says the one who holds the seven stars in his right hand and who walks among the seven golden lampstands: [2] I know your works, your labor, and your endurance, and that you cannot tolerate evil people. You have tested those who call themselves apostles and are not, and you have found them to be liars. [3] I know that you have persevered and endured hardships for the sake of my name, and you have not grown weary. [4] But I have this against you: You have abandoned the love you had at first. [5] Remember then how far you have fallen; repent, and do the works you did at first. Otherwise, I will come to you and remove your lampstand from its place, unless you repent."

## REVELATION 3:1–4, 14–20
### The Letter to Sardis

[1] "Write to the angel of the church in Sardis: Thus says the one who has the seven spirits of God and the seven stars: I know your works; you have a reputation for being alive, but you are dead. [2] Be alert and strengthen what remains, which is about to die, for I have not found your works complete before my God. [3] Remember, then, what you have received and heard; keep it, and repent. If you are not alert, I will come like a thief, and you have no idea at what hour I will come upon you. [4] But you have a few people in Sardis who have not defiled their clothes, and they will walk with me in white, because they are worthy."

…

### The Letter to Laodicea

[14] "Write to the angel of the church in Laodicea: Thus says the Amen, the faithful and true witness, the originator of God's creation: [15] I know your works, that you are neither cold nor hot. I wish that you were cold or hot. [16] So, because you are lukewarm, and neither hot nor cold, I am going to vomit you out of my mouth. [17] For you say, 'I'm rich; I have become wealthy and need nothing,' and you don't realize that you are wretched, pitiful, poor, blind, and naked. [18] I advise you to buy from me gold refined in the fire so that you may be rich, white clothes so that you may be dressed and your shameful nakedness not be exposed, and ointment to spread on your eyes so that you may see. [19] As many as I love, I rebuke and discipline. So be zealous and repent. [20] See! I stand at the door and knock. If anyone hears my voice and opens the door, I will come in to him and eat with him, and he with me."

## 2 CORINTHIANS 3:18
We all, with unveiled faces, are looking as in a mirror at the glory of the Lord and are being transformed into the same image from glory to glory; this is from the Lord who is the Spirit.

## DANIEL 9:3–10, 17–19

[3] So I turned my attention to the Lord God to seek him by prayer and petitions, with fasting, sackcloth, and ashes.

[4] I prayed to the LORD my God and confessed:

Ah, Lord—the great and awe-inspiring God who keeps his gracious covenant with those who love him and keep his commands— [5] we have sinned, done wrong, acted wickedly, rebelled, and turned away from your commands and ordinances. [6] We have not listened to your servants the prophets, who spoke in your name to our kings, leaders, ancestors, and all the people of the land.

[7] Lord, righteousness belongs to you, but this day public shame belongs to us: the men of Judah, the residents of Jerusalem, and all Israel—those who are near and those who are far, in all the countries where you have banished them because of the disloyalty they have shown toward you. [8] LORD, public shame belongs to us, our kings, our leaders, and our ancestors, because we have sinned against you. [9] Compassion and forgiveness belong to the Lord our God, though we have rebelled against him [10] and have not obeyed the LORD our God by following his instructions that he set before us through his servants the prophets.

…

[17] Therefore, our God, hear the prayer and the petitions of your servant. Make your face shine on your desolate sanctuary for the Lord's sake. [18] Listen closely, my God, and hear. Open your eyes and see our desolations and the city that bears your name. For we are not presenting our petitions before you based on our righteous acts, but based on your abundant compassion. [19] Lord, hear! Lord, forgive! Lord, listen and act! My God, for your own sake, do not delay, because your city and your people bear your name.

## PSALM 51:1–6, 10–17

*A Prayer for Restoration*

*For the choir director. A psalm of David, when the prophet Nathan came to him after he had gone to Bathsheba.*

[1] Be gracious to me, God,
according to your faithful love;
according to your abundant compassion,
blot out my rebellion.
[2] Completely wash away my guilt
and cleanse me from my sin.
[3] For I am conscious of my rebellion,
and my sin is always before me.

⁴ Against you—you alone—I have sinned
and done this evil in your sight.
So you are right when you pass sentence;
you are blameless when you judge.
⁵ Indeed, I was guilty when I was born;
I was sinful when my mother conceived me.

⁶ Surely you desire integrity in the inner self,
and you teach me wisdom deep within.

…

¹⁰ God, create a clean heart for me
and renew a steadfast spirit within me.

¹¹ Do not banish me from your presence
or take your Holy Spirit from me.
¹² Restore the joy of your salvation to me,
and sustain me by giving me a willing spirit.
¹³ Then I will teach the rebellious your ways,
and sinners will return to you.

¹⁴ Save me from the guilt of bloodshed, God—
God of my salvation—
and my tongue will sing of your righteousness.
¹⁵ Lord, open my lips,
and my mouth will declare your praise.
¹⁶ You do not want a sacrifice, or I would give it;
you are not pleased with a burnt offering.
¹⁷ The sacrifice pleasing to God is a broken spirit.
You will not despise a broken and humbled heart, God.

*The Church is*

# RECONCILED TO GOD AND ONE ANOTHER

*Because the Church is a people reconciled to God in Christ, believers can also be reconciled to one another as evidence of the hope found in Him.*

## EPHESIANS 2:11–18
*Unity in Christ*

¹¹ So, then, remember that at one time you were Gentiles in the flesh—called "the uncircumcised" by those called "the circumcised," which is done in the flesh by human hands. ¹² At that time you were without Christ, excluded from the citizenship of Israel, and foreigners to the covenants of promise, without hope and without God in the world. ¹³ But now in Christ Jesus, you who were far away have been brought near by the blood of Christ. ¹⁴ For he is our peace, who made both groups one and tore down the dividing wall of hostility. In his flesh, ¹⁵ he made of no effect the law consisting of commands and expressed in regulations, so that he might create in himself one new man from the two, resulting in peace. ¹⁶ He did this so that he might reconcile both to God in one body through the cross by which he put the hostility to death. ¹⁷ He came and proclaimed the good news of peace to you who were far away and peace to those who were near. ¹⁸ For through him we both have access in one Spirit to the Father.

## 2 CORINTHIANS 5:18–20

¹⁸ Everything is from God, who has reconciled us to himself through Christ and has given us the ministry of reconciliation.

¹⁹ That is, in Christ, God was reconciling the world to himself, not counting their trespasses against them, and he has committed the message of reconciliation to us.

²⁰ Therefore, we are ambassadors for Christ, since God is making his appeal through us. We plead on Christ's behalf, "Be reconciled to God."

## MATTHEW 18:15–20
*Restoring a Brother*

¹⁵ "If your brother sins against you, go tell him his fault, between you and him alone. If he listens to you, you have won your brother. ¹⁶ But if he won't listen, take one or two others with you, so that by the testimony of two or three witnesses every fact may be established. ¹⁷ If he doesn't pay attention to them, tell the church. If he doesn't pay attention even to the church, let him be like a Gentile and a tax collector to you. ¹⁸ Truly I tell you, whatever you bind on earth will have been bound in heaven, and whatever you loose on earth will have been loosed in heaven. ¹⁹ Again, truly I tell you, if two of you on earth agree about any matter that you pray for, it will be done for you by my Father in heaven. ²⁰ For where two or three are gathered together in my name, I am there among them."

COLOSSIANS 1:19–23

¹⁹ For God was pleased to have
all his fullness dwell in him,
²⁰ and through him to reconcile
everything to himself,
whether things on earth or things in heaven,
by making peace
through his blood, shed on the cross.

²¹ Once you were alienated and hostile in your minds as expressed in your evil actions. ²² But now he has reconciled you by his physical body through his death, to present you holy, faultless, and blameless before him— ²³ if indeed you remain grounded and steadfast in the faith and are not shifted away from the hope of the gospel that you heard. This gospel has been proclaimed in all creation under heaven, and I, Paul, have become a servant of it.

2 CORINTHIANS 3:1–6

*Living Letters*

¹ Are we beginning to commend ourselves again? Or do we need, like some, letters of recommendation to you or from you? ² You yourselves are our letter, written on our hearts, known and read by everyone. ³ You show that you are Christ's letter, delivered by us, not written with ink but with the Spirit of the living God—not on tablets of stone but on tablets of human hearts.

*Paul's Competence*

⁴ Such is the confidence we have through Christ before God. ⁵ It is not that we are competent in ourselves to claim anything as coming from ourselves, but our adequacy is from God. ⁶ He has made us competent to be ministers of a new covenant, not of the letter, but of the Spirit. For the letter kills, but the Spirit gives life.

# A SHEPHERDED FLOCK

*Day 32*

*Christ calls believers to tend, care for, guide, and serve the Church. Leaders are called to a high standard of character and behavior as undershepherds responsible to Christ for how they care for His sheep.*

## JOHN 21:15–17
*Jesus's Threefold Restoration of Peter*

[15] When they had eaten breakfast, Jesus asked Simon Peter, "Simon, son of John, do you love me more than these?"

"Yes, Lord," he said to him, "you know that I love you."

"Feed my lambs," he told him. [16] A second time he asked him, "Simon, son of John, do you love me?"

"Yes, Lord," he said to him, "you know that I love you."

"Shepherd my sheep," he told him.

[17] He asked him the third time, "Simon, son of John, do you love me?"

Peter was grieved that he asked him the third time, "Do you love me?" He said, "Lord, you know everything; you know that I love you."

"Feed my sheep," Jesus said.

## MATTHEW 20:20–28
*Suffering and Service*

[20] Then the mother of Zebedee's sons approached him with her sons. She knelt down to ask him for something. [21] "What do you want?" he asked her.

"Promise," she said to him, "that these two sons of mine may sit, one on your right and the other on your left, in your kingdom."

<sup>22</sup> Jesus answered, "You don't know what you're asking. Are you able to drink the cup that I am about to drink?"

"We are able," they said to him.

<sup>23</sup> He told them, "You will indeed drink my cup, but to sit at my right and left is not mine to give; instead, it is for those for whom it has been prepared by my Father."

<sup>24</sup> When the ten disciples heard this, they became indignant with the two brothers. <sup>25</sup> Jesus called them over and said, "You know that the rulers of the Gentiles lord it over them, and those in high positions act as tyrants over them. <sup>26</sup> It must not be like that among you. On the contrary, whoever wants to become great among you must be your servant, <sup>27</sup> and whoever wants to be first among you must be your slave; <sup>28</sup> just as the Son of Man did not come to be served, but to serve, and to give his life as a ransom for many."

## EPHESIANS 4:11-14

<sup>11</sup> And he himself gave some to be apostles, some prophets, some evangelists, some pastors and teachers, <sup>12</sup> to equip the saints for the work of ministry, to build up the body of Christ, <sup>13</sup> until we all reach unity in the faith and in the knowledge of God's Son, growing into maturity with a stature measured by Christ's fullness. <sup>14</sup> Then we will no longer be little children, tossed by the waves and blown around by every wind of teaching, by human cunning with cleverness in the techniques of deceit.

## 1 PETER 5:1-5
*About the Elders*

<sup>1</sup> I exhort the elders among you as a fellow elder and witness to the sufferings of Christ, as well as one who shares in the glory about to be revealed: <sup>2</sup> Shepherd God's flock among you, not overseeing out of compulsion but willingly, as God would have you; not out of greed for money but eagerly;

<sup>3</sup> not lording it over those entrusted to you, but being examples to the flock.

<sup>4</sup> And when the chief Shepherd appears, you will receive the unfading crown of glory. <sup>5</sup> In the same way, you who are younger, be subject to the elders. All of you clothe yourselves with humility toward one another, because

God resists the proud
but gives grace to the humble.

## ACTS 6:1-6
*Seven Chosen to Serve*

<sup>1</sup> In those days, as the disciples were increasing in number, there arose a complaint by the Hellenistic Jews against the Hebraic Jews that their widows were being overlooked in the daily distribution. <sup>2</sup> The Twelve summoned the whole company of the disciples and said, "It would not be right for us to give up preaching the word of God to wait on tables. <sup>3</sup> Brothers and sisters, select from among you seven men of good reputation, full of the Spirit and wisdom, whom we can appoint to this duty. <sup>4</sup> But we will devote ourselves to prayer and to the ministry of the word." <sup>5</sup> This proposal pleased the whole company. So they chose Stephen, a man full of faith and the Holy Spirit, and Philip, Prochorus, Nicanor, Timon, Parmenas, and Nicolaus, a convert from Antioch. <sup>6</sup> They had them stand before the apostles, who prayed and laid their hands on them.

## ACTS 20:28-31

<sup>28</sup> Be on guard for yourselves and for all the flock of which the Holy Spirit has appointed you as overseers, to shepherd the church of God, which he purchased with his own blood. <sup>29</sup> I know that after my departure savage wolves will come in among you, not sparing the flock. <sup>30</sup> Men will rise up even from your own number and distort the truth to lure the disciples into following them. <sup>31</sup> Therefore be on the alert, remembering that night and day for three years I never stopped warning each one of you with tears.

## 1 TIMOTHY 3:1-13 NIV
*Qualifications for Overseers and Deacons*

<sup>1</sup> Here is a trustworthy saying: Whoever aspires to be an overseer desires a noble task. <sup>2</sup> Now the overseer is to

# Approaches to Church Government

At She Reads Truth, our primary goal is to invite and equip you to read the Bible. Today's readings are passages on leadership within the Church. Across the spectrum of Christianity, local church communities operate under the day-to-day leadership of believers. Traditions that faithfully follow Jesus and uphold the authority of Scripture differ in interpretation about how the local church should be structured, organized, and held accountable. Below are brief summaries of three broad approaches to church structure.

---

**EPISCOPALIAN FORM**

This structure centers on a hierarchy where a bishop oversees a number of pastors serving individual congregations. These bishops are in turn accountable to an archbishop or to a larger committee.

---

**PRESBYTERIAN FORM**

A number of teaching and leading elders from multiple local congregations make up a regional committee, called a presbytery, that has ruling authority over churches in its area and its members.

---

**CONGREGATIONALIST FORM**

These churches are democratically led by the congregation and elected officers. They function independently and autonomously, though many congregationalist churches are part of larger cooperative associations.

SCRIPTURES ABOUT CHURCH GOVERNMENT

*Acts 6:1–6; 20:28–31; Ephesians 4:11–14; 1 Thessalonians 5:12–13; 1 Timothy 3:1–13; Titus 1:5–9; Hebrews 13:7, 17; 1 Peter 5:1–5*

be above reproach, faithful to his wife, temperate, self-controlled, respectable, hospitable, able to teach, ³ not given to drunkenness, not violent but gentle, not quarrelsome, not a lover of money. ⁴ He must manage his own family well and see that his children obey him, and he must do so in a manner worthy of full respect. ⁵ (If anyone does not know how to manage his own family, how can he take care of God's church?) ⁶ He must not be a recent convert, or he may become conceited and fall under the same judgment as the devil.

## ⁷ He must also have a good reputation with outsiders, so that he will not fall into disgrace and into the devil's trap.

⁸ In the same way, deacons are to be worthy of respect, sincere, not indulging in much wine, and not pursuing dishonest gain. ⁹ They must keep hold of the deep truths of the faith with a clear conscience. ¹⁰ They must first be tested; and then if there is nothing against them, let them serve as deacons.

¹¹ In the same way, the women are to be worthy of respect, not malicious talkers but temperate and trustworthy in everything.

¹² A deacon must be faithful to his wife and must manage his children and his household well. ¹³ Those who have served well gain an excellent standing and great assurance in their faith in Christ Jesus.

### PROVERBS 11:14

Without guidance, a people will fall,
but with many counselors there is deliverance.

### TITUS 1:5-9

*Titus's Ministry in Crete*

⁵ The reason I left you in Crete was to set right what was left undone and, as I directed you, to appoint elders in every town. ⁶ An elder must be blameless, the husband of one wife, with faithful children who are not accused of wildness or rebellion. ⁷ As an overseer of God's household, he must be blameless, not arrogant, not hot-tempered, not an excessive drinker, not a bully, not greedy for money, ⁸ but hospitable, loving what is good, sensible, righteous, holy, self-controlled, ⁹ holding to the faithful message as taught, so that he will be able both to encourage with sound teaching and to refute those who contradict it.

### HEBREWS 13:7, 17

⁷ Remember your leaders who have spoken God's word to you. As you carefully observe the outcome of their lives, imitate their faith.

. . .

¹⁷ Obey your leaders and submit to them, since they keep watch over your souls as those who will give an account, so that they can do this with joy and not with grief, for that would be unprofitable for you.

### 1 THESSALONIANS 5:12-13

¹² Now we ask you, brothers and sisters, to give recognition to those who labor among you and lead you in the Lord and admonish you, ¹³ and to regard them very highly in love because of their work. Be at peace among yourselves.

THE CHURCH IS

# A PERSEVERING
# PEOPLE

*Despite persecution, internal conflict, shortcomings, sin, rejection, and suffering, the Church endures because it is Christ who sustains it.*

*Day 33*

[19] "If you were of the world, the world would love you as its own. However, because you are not of the world, but I have chosen you out of it, the world hates you. [20] Remember the word I spoke to you: 'A servant is not greater than his master.' If they persecuted me, they will also persecute you. If they kept my word, they will also keep yours."

ACTS 4:1–20

*Peter and John Arrested*

[1] While they were speaking to the people, the priests, the captain of the temple police, and the Sadducees confronted them, [2] because they were annoyed that they were teaching the people and proclaiming in Jesus the resurrection of the dead. [3] So they seized them and took them into custody until the next day since it was already evening. [4] But many of those who heard the message believed, and the number of the men came to about five thousand.

*Peter and John Face the Jewish Leadership*

[5] The next day, their rulers, elders, and scribes assembled in Jerusalem [6] with Annas the high priest, Caiaphas, John, Alexander, and all the members of the high-priestly family. [7] After they had Peter and John stand before them, they began to question them: "By what power or in what name have you done this?"

[8] Then Peter was filled with the Holy Spirit and said to them, "Rulers of the people and elders: [9] If we are being examined today about a good deed done to a disabled man, by what means he was healed, [10] let it be known to all of you and to all the people of Israel, that by the name of Jesus Christ of Nazareth, whom you crucified and whom God raised from the dead—by him this man is standing here before you healthy. [11] This Jesus is

the stone rejected by you builders,
which has become the cornerstone.

[12] There is salvation in no one else, for there is no other name under heaven given to people by which we must be saved."

*The Boldness of the Disciples*

[13] When they observed the boldness of Peter and John and realized that they were uneducated and untrained men, they were amazed and recognized that they had been with Jesus. [14] And since they saw the man who had been healed standing with them, they had nothing to say in opposition. [15] After they ordered them to leave the Sanhedrin, they conferred among themselves, [16] saying, "What should we do with these men? For an obvious sign has been done through them, clear to everyone living in Jerusalem, and we cannot deny it. [17] But so that this does not spread any further among the people, let's threaten them against speaking to anyone in this name again." [18] So they called for them and ordered them not to speak or teach at all in the name of Jesus.

[19] Peter and John answered them, "Whether it's right in the sight of God for us to listen to you rather than to God, you decide; [20] for we are unable to stop speaking about what we have seen and heard."

1 PETER 4:12–14

*Christian Suffering*

[12] Dear friends, don't be surprised when the fiery ordeal comes among you to test you, as if something unusual were happening to you. [13] Instead, rejoice as you share in the sufferings of Christ, so that you may also rejoice with great joy when his glory is revealed. [14] If you are ridiculed for the name of Christ, you are blessed, because the Spirit of glory and of God rests on you.

1 PETER 5:8

Be sober-minded, be alert. Your adversary the devil is prowling around like a roaring lion, looking for anyone he can devour.

EPHESIANS 6:10–12

*Christian Warfare*

[10] Finally, be strengthened by the Lord and by his vast strength. [11] Put on the full armor of God so that you can stand against the schemes of the devil. [12] For our struggle is

not against flesh and blood, but against the rulers, against the authorities, against the cosmic powers of this darkness, against evil, spiritual forces in the heavens.

## 2 CORINTHIANS 4:7–10
### Treasure in Clay Jars

[7] Now we have this treasure in clay jars, so that this extraordinary power may be from God and not from us. [8] We are afflicted in every way but not crushed; we are perplexed but not in despair; [9] we are persecuted but not abandoned; we are struck down but not destroyed. [10] We always carry the death of Jesus in our body, so that the life of Jesus may also be displayed in our body.

## JAMES 1:2–4
### Trials and Maturity

[2] Consider it a great joy, my brothers and sisters, whenever you experience various trials, [3] because you know that the testing of your faith produces endurance. [4] And let endurance have its full effect, so that you may be mature and complete, lacking nothing.

## REVELATION 1:4–6

[4] John: To the seven churches in Asia. Grace and peace to you from the one who is, who was, and who is to come, and from the seven spirits before his throne, [5] and from Jesus Christ, the faithful witness, the firstborn from the dead and the ruler of the kings of the earth.

To him who loves us and has set us free from our sins by his blood, [6] and made us a kingdom, priests to his God and Father—to him be glory and dominion forever and ever. Amen.

## REVELATION 12:7–11
### The Dragon Thrown Out of Heaven

[7] Then war broke out in heaven: Michael and his angels fought against the dragon. The dragon and his angels also fought, [8] but he could not prevail, and there was no place for them in heaven any longer. [9] So the great dragon was thrown out—the ancient serpent, who is called the devil and Satan, the one who deceives the whole world. He was thrown to earth, and his angels with him. [10] Then I heard a loud voice in heaven say,

The salvation and the power
and the kingdom of our God
and the authority of his Christ
have now come,
because the accuser of our brothers and sisters,
who accuses them
before our God day and night,
has been thrown down.
[11] They conquered him
by the blood of the Lamb
and by the word of their testimony;
for they did not love their lives
to the point of death.

## ROMANS 8:31–39
### The Believer's Triumph

[31] What, then, are we to say about these things? If God is for us, who is against us? [32] He did not even spare his own Son but gave him up for us all. How will he not also with him grant us everything? [33] Who can bring an accusation against God's elect? God is the one who justifies. [34] Who is the one who condemns? Christ Jesus is the one who died, but even more, has been raised; he also is at the right hand of God and intercedes for us. [35] Who can separate us from the love of Christ? Can affliction or distress or persecution or famine or nakedness or danger or sword? [36] As it is written:

Because of you
we are being put to death all day long;
we are counted as sheep to be slaughtered.

[37] No, in all these things we are more than conquerors through him who loved us. [38] For I am persuaded that neither death nor life, nor angels nor rulers, nor things present nor things to come, nor powers, [39] nor height nor depth, nor any other created thing will be able to separate us from the love of God that is in Christ Jesus our Lord.

# Notes

_Date_

# THE
# PERSECUTION
# OF GOD'S PEOPLE

*in Scripture*

Scripture shows us that God's people face persecution and oppression. In this suffering, God continues to display His faithfulness in making and preserving a people for Himself. The chart on the following pages provides a glimpse into some moments in biblical history where God's people experienced His faithfulness amid persecution and oppression.

The persecution and oppression of God's people still exists globally today. Reflect on God's faithfulness and spend time in prayer for your brothers and sisters around the world.

| | *Persecution and Oppression* | *God's Faithfulness to His People* |
|---|---|---|
| In Egypt, Israel continued to multiply despite Pharoah's determined oppression. | "Look, the Israelite people are more numerous and powerful than we are. Come, let's deal shrewdly with them; otherwise they will multiply further, and when war breaks out, they will join our enemies, fight against us, and leave the country." So the Egyptians assigned taskmasters over the Israelites to oppress them with forced labor.<br><br>EXODUS 1:9–11 | But the more they oppressed them, the more they multiplied and spread so that the Egyptians came to dread the Israelites.<br><br>EXODUS 1:12 |
| God protected the Jewish people in the face of Haman's destructive plot. | Then Haman informed King Ahasuerus, "There is one ethnic group, scattered throughout the peoples in every province of your kingdom, keeping themselves separate. Their laws are different from everyone else's and they do not obey the king's laws. It is not in the king's best interest to tolerate them. If the king approves, let an order be drawn up authorizing their destruction, and I will pay 375 tons of silver to the officials for deposit in the royal treasury."<br><br>ESTHER 3:8–9 | On the day when the Jews' enemies had hoped to overpower them, just the opposite happened. The Jews overpowered those who hated them.<br><br>ESTHER 9:1 |

Through God's provision, the Jewish people were able to finish rebuilding the wall around Jerusalem that had been destroyed by the Babylonians.

And our enemies said, "They won't realize it until we're among them and can kill them and stop the work." When the Jews who lived nearby arrived, they said to us time and again, "Everywhere you turn, they attack us."

NEHEMIAH 4:11–12

The wall was completed in fifty-two days, on the twenty-fifth day of the month Elul. When all our enemies heard this, all the surrounding nations were intimidated and lost their confidence, for they realized that this task had been accomplished by our God.

NEHEMIAH 6:15–16

While in exile, God's people faced persecution when they refused to worship another god. God delivered them from their enemy's threats.

Some Chaldeans took this occasion to come forward and maliciously accuse the Jews. They said to King Nebuchadnezzar, "May the king live forever. You as king have issued a decree that everyone who hears the sound of the horn, flute, zither, lyre, harp, drum, and every kind of music must fall down and worship the gold statue. Whoever does not fall down and worship will be thrown into a furnace of blazing fire. There are some Jews you have appointed to manage the province of Babylon: Shadrach, Meshach, and Abednego. These men have ignored you, the king; they do not serve your gods or worship the gold statue you have set up."

…

Then Nebuchadnezzar was filled with rage, and the expression on his face changed toward Shadrach, Meshach, and Abednego. He gave orders to heat the furnace seven times more than was customary, and he commanded some of the best soldiers in his army to tie up Shadrach, Meshach, and Abednego and throw them into the furnace of blazing fire.

DANIEL 3:8–12, 19–20

Nebuchadnezzar then approached the door of the furnace of blazing fire and called, "Shadrach, Meshach, and Abednego, you servants of the Most High God—come out!" So Shadrach, Meshach, and Abednego came out of the fire. When the satraps, prefects, governors, and the king's advisers gathered around, they saw that the fire had no effect on the bodies of these men: not a hair of their heads was singed, their robes were unaffected, and there was no smell of fire on them. Nebuchadnezzar exclaimed, "Praise to the God of Shadrach, Meshach, and Abednego! He sent his angel and rescued his servants who trusted in him. They violated the king's command and risked their lives rather than serve or worship any god except their own God."

DANIEL 3:26–28

In the early Church, the number of Christians continued to grow in the face of opposition.

While they were speaking to the people, the priests, the captain of the temple police, and the Sadducees confronted them, because they were annoyed that they were teaching the people and proclaiming in Jesus the resurrection of the dead. So they seized them and took them into custody until the next day since it was already evening.

ACTS 4:1–3

But many of those who heard the message believed, and the number of the men came to about five thousand.

ACTS 4:4

As the early Church scattered in response to persecution, they spread the good news of Jesus wherever they went.

A severe persecution broke out against the church in Jerusalem, and all except the apostles were scattered throughout the land of Judea and Samaria. Devout men buried Stephen and mourned deeply over him. Saul, however, was ravaging the church. He would enter house after house, drag off men and women, and put them in prison.

ACTS 8:1–3

So those who were scattered went on their way preaching the word.

ACTS 8:4

WEEK 5

# RESPONSE

*The Church is...*

CALLED TO PRAYER

A PEOPLE IN PROGRESS

RECONCILED TO GOD
AND ONE ANOTHER

A SHEPHERDED FLOCK

A PERSEVERING PEOPLE

Use these questions as a guide for reflecting
on this week's reading. You may not have a
response for each one—that's okay!

What truths about the
Church stood out to you?

_____

What comforted or
encouraged you?

_____

What challenged you?

_____

What questions do you have
that you want to explore?

_____

What action might you need
to take in response to what
you read this week? What is
your first step?

_____

1

2

3

4

5

# Grace Day

*Take this day to catch up on your reading, pray, and rest in the presence of the Lord.*

LORD, HEAR! LORD, FORGIVE! LORD, LISTEN AND ACT! MY GOD, FOR YOUR OWN SAKE, DO NOT DELAY, BECAUSE YOUR CITY AND YOUR PEOPLE BEAR YOUR NAME.

*Daniel 9:19*

DAY 35

*Weekly Truth*

Scripture is God-breathed and true. When we memorize it,
we carry the good news of Jesus with us wherever we go.

During our time in this study, we have worked to memorize
Ephesians 4:1–6. Spend some time reviewing the full passage as a
reminder of the beauty of God's Church.

Therefore I, the prisoner in the Lord, urge you to walk worthy of the calling you have received, with all humility and gentleness, with patience, bearing with one another in love, making every effort to keep the unity of the Spirit through the bond of peace. There is one body and one Spirit—just as you were called to one hope at your calling—one Lord, one faith, one baptism, one God and Father of all, who is above all and through all and in all.

EPHESIANS 4:1–6

*See tips for memorizing Scripture on page 182.*

BENEDICTION

Now to him who is able to do above and beyond all that we ask or think according to the power that works in us—to him be glory in the church and in Christ Jesus to all generations, forever and ever. Amen.

*Ephesians 3:20–21*

# FURTHER READING

SHE READS TRUTH STUDY BOOKS

*Acts*

*Faith in Practice:*
*A Biblical Study of Spiritual Disciplines*

*In Spirit and in Truth:*
*A Study of Biblical Worship*

*The Kingdom of God*

*Making Room:*
*A Study of Biblical Hospitality*

*One Another:*
*A Biblical Study of Christian Community*

*This Is the Gospel*

We believe our faith is meant to be lived out in community with other believers. Ask your local pastor and spiritual community for their recommended resources on both the global Church and your specific church tradition.

Here is a brief list of additional resources from a variety of perspectives within the Christian faith that have challenged, encouraged, or provided insight on different traditions for members of our team.

*A Multitude of All Peoples*
by Vince L. Bantu

*Evangelical Theology 2nd ed.*
by Michael F. Bird

*Life Together*
by Dietrich Bonhoeffer

*Oneness Embraced*
by Tony Evans

*Streams of Living Water*
by Richard J. Foster

*The Story of Christianity*
by Justo L. González

*When the Church Was a Family*
by Joseph H. Hellerman

*Church in Ordinary Time*
by Amy Plantinga Pauw

*Readings in the History of Christian Theology*
by William C. Placher

*The Emotionally Healthy Church*
by Pete Scazzero

*Church History in Plain Language*
by Bruce L. Shelley

*Desiring the Kingdom (Cultural Liturgies Volume 1)*
by James K. A. Smith

*The Great Omission*
by Dallas Willard

*Surprised by Hope*
by N. T. Wright

*The Counterpoints: Bible & Theology Series*
from Zondervan Academic

# Tips for Memorizing Scripture

At She Reads Truth, we believe Scripture memorization is an important discipline in your walk with God. Committing God's Truth to memory means He can minister to us—and we can minister to others—through His Word no matter where we are. As you approach the Weekly Truth passage in this book, try these memorization tips to see which techniques work best for you!

**STUDY IT**

Study the passage in its biblical context and ask yourself a few questions before you begin to memorize it: What does this passage say? What does it mean? How would I say this in my own words? What does it teach me about God? Understanding what the passage means helps you know why it is important to carry it with you wherever you go.

Break the passage into smaller sections, memorizing a phrase at a time.

**PRAY IT**

Use the passage you are memorizing as a prompt for prayer.

**WRITE IT**

Dedicate a notebook to Scripture memorization and write the passage over and over again.

Diagram the passage after you write it out. Place a square around the verbs, underline the nouns, and circle any adjectives or adverbs. Say the passage aloud several times, emphasizing the verbs as you repeat it. Then do the same thing again with the nouns, then the adjectives and adverbs.

Write out the first letter of each word in the passage somewhere you can reference it throughout the week as you work on your memorization.

Use a whiteboard to write out the passage. Erase a few words at a time as you continue to repeat it aloud. Keep erasing parts of the passage until you have it all committed to memory.

**CREATE**

If you can, make up a tune for the passage to sing as you go about your day, or try singing it to the tune of a favorite song.

Sketch the passage, visualizing what each phrase would look like in the form of a picture. Or, try using calligraphy or altering the style of your handwriting as you write it out.

Use hand signals or signs to come up with associations for each word or phrase and repeat the movements as you practice.

**SAY IT**

Repeat the passage out loud to yourself as you are going through the rhythm of your day—getting ready, pouring your coffee, waiting in traffic, or making dinner.

Listen to the passage read aloud to you.

Record a voice memo on your phone and listen to it throughout the day or play it on an audio Bible.

**SHARE IT**

Memorize the passage with a friend, family member, or mentor. Spontaneously challenge each other to recite the passage, or pick a time to review your passage and practice saying it from memory together.

Send the passage as an encouraging text to a friend, testing yourself as you type to see how much you have memorized so far.

**KEEP AT IT!**

Set reminders on your phone to prompt you to practice your passage.

Purchase a She Reads Truth 12 Card Set or keep a stack of notecards with Scripture you are memorizing by your bed. Practice reciting what you've memorized previously before you go to sleep, ending with the passages you are currently learning. If you wake up in the middle of the night, review them again instead of grabbing your phone. Read them out loud before you get out of bed in the morning.

Download the free Weekly Truth lock screens for your phone on the She Reads Truth app and read the passage throughout the day when you check your phone.

## CSB BOOK ABBREVIATIONS

### OLD TESTAMENT

| | | | | | | | |
|---|---|---|---|---|---|---|---|
| **GN** Genesis | | **JB** Job | | **HAB** Habakkuk | | **PHP** Philippians | |
| **EX** Exodus | | **PS** Psalms | | **ZPH** Zephaniah | | **COL** Colossians | |
| **LV** Leviticus | | **PR** Proverbs | | **HG** Haggai | | **1TH** 1 Thessalonians | |
| **NM** Numbers | | **EC** Ecclesiastes | | **ZCH** Zechariah | | **2TH** 2 Thessalonians | |
| **DT** Deuteronomy | | **SG** Song of Solomon | | **MAL** Malachi | | **1TM** 1 Timothy | |
| **JOS** Joshua | | **IS** Isaiah | | | | **2TM** 2 Timothy | |
| **JDG** Judges | | **JR** Jeremiah | | **NEW TESTAMENT** | | **TI** Titus | |
| **RU** Ruth | | **LM** Lamentations | | **MT** Matthew | | **PHM** Philemon | |
| **1SM** 1 Samuel | | **EZK** Ezekiel | | **MK** Mark | | **HEB** Hebrews | |
| **2SM** 2 Samuel | | **DN** Daniel | | **LK** Luke | | **JMS** James | |
| **1KG** 1 Kings | | **HS** Hosea | | **JN** John | | **1PT** 1 Peter | |
| **2KG** 2 Kings | | **JL** Joel | | **AC** Acts | | **2PT** 2 Peter | |
| **1CH** 1 Chronicles | | **AM** Amos | | **RM** Romans | | **1JN** 1 John | |
| **2CH** 2 Chronicles | | **OB** Obadiah | | **1CO** 1 Corinthians | | **2JN** 2 John | |
| **EZR** Ezra | | **JNH** Jonah | | **2CO** 2 Corinthians | | **3JN** 3 John | |
| **NEH** Nehemiah | | **MC** Micah | | **GL** Galatians | | **JD** Jude | |
| **EST** Esther | | **NAH** Nahum | | **EPH** Ephesians | | **RV** Revelation | |

---

## BIBLIOGRAPHY

Alikin, Valeriy A. "The Reading of Scripture in the Gathering of the Early Church," *The Earliest History of the Christian Gathering: Origin, Development and Content of the Christian Gathering in the First to Third Centuries*, 102 (2010): 147–182. https://doi.org/10.1163/ej.9789004183094.i-342.28.

Bird, Michael F. *Evangelical Theology: A Biblical and Systematic Introduction.* 2nd ed. Grand Rapids: Zondervan Academic, 2020.

Blomberg, Craig L. *Jesus and the Gospels: An Introduction and Survey.* 2nd ed. Nashville: B&H Academic, 2009.

Bonhoeffer, Dietrich. *Life Together.* New York: Harper Collins, 1954.

Clowney, Edmund P. *The Church: Contours of Christian Theology.* Downers Grove: InterVarsity Press, 1995.

Jenson, Matt and David Wilhite. *The Church: A Guide for the Perplexed.* London: T&T Clark International, 2010.

Lloyd-Jones, D. Martyn. *Revival.* Wheaton, IL: Crossway, 1987.

Osei-Bonsu, Robert. "The Church as the *People of God* and Its Relation to the Church as a Community." *Asian-Africa Journal of Mission & Ministry,* 4 (2011): 57–73.

Stott, John. *The Cross of Christ.* Downers Grove: InterVarsity Press, 2021.

Tozer, Aiden W. *Keys to the Deeper Life.* Grand Rapids: Zondervan, 1957.

*World Christian Encyclopedia.* 3rd ed. Edited by Todd M. Johnson and Gina A. Zurio. Edinburgh: Edinburgh University Press, 2019.

Wright, Christopher. *The Mission of God's People: A Biblical Theology of the Church's Mission.* Biblical Theology for Life. Grand Rapids: Zondervan, 2010.

# Never miss a day in God's Word.

The **She Reads Truth Subscription Box** is an easy way to have a Bible reading plan for every day of the year.

Every month, we'll send you a new Study Book filled with daily Scripture readings and all sorts of beautiful extra features to help you read and understand the Bible. All you have to do is open your book, read with us today, and read with us again tomorrow—it's that simple!

SHEREADSTRUTH.COM/SUBBOX

# You just spent 35 days in the Word of God!

MY FAVORITE DAY OF
THIS READING PLAN:

HOW DID I FIND DELIGHT IN GOD'S WORD?

ONE THING I LEARNED
ABOUT GOD:

WHAT WAS GOD DOING IN
MY LIFE DURING THIS STUDY?

WHAT DID I LEARN THAT I WANT TO SHARE
WITH SOMEONE ELSE?

A SPECIFIC SCRIPTURE THAT
ENCOURAGED ME:

A SPECIFIC SCRIPTURE THAT
CHALLENGED AND CONVICTED ME: